DECORATIVE FURNITURE FINISHES

WITH Vinegar Paint

BILL RUSSELL

NORTH LIGHT BOOKS
CINCINNATI, OHIO

ABOUT THE AUTHOR

 Bill Russell was born, raised and educated in Ohio, completing degrees in art at Kent State University in Kent, Ohio and at Miami University in Oxford, Ohio. He has taught art in a variety of settings, to students of all ages and degrees of sophistication. He currently teaches drawing at the Philadelphia College of Textiles and Science, in addition to operating his own studio and gallery, where he offers a series of decorative arts workshops.

Bill worked for a number of years in antique restoration and refinishing. It was his dual interests in painting and furniture that led to his involvement with painted finishes for furniture. In addition to painted furniture, Bill has exhibited artwork in a variety of mediums at galleries and museums throughout the United States. His vinegar painted work was also featured in *Country Living* magazine.

Bill and his wife, Mary Galgon, have two sons, Miles and Ian. They reside in center city Philadelphia.

ACKNOWLEDGMENTS

I would like to acknowledge and thank several people who have helped to make this book possible: my longtime friend, Randy Starkie, who facilitated my connection with North Light Books; my studio assistants, Scott Slezak, Joni Fitzgerald and more recently, Ken Chernishchenko, who helped prepare the furniture shown in this book; and my photographer, Greg Benson, who contributed not only his skill and creativity but lots of great advice. My clients and students deserve thanks for pushing me to explore more complex techniques. I also want to thank Allen and Ina Marx of The Finishing School and all my other teachers over the years who have shared their knowledge and time. I would like to acknowledge the community of furniture artists of the Philadelphia area whose dedication to high standards and creativity have provided ongoing inspiration. Finally, I would like to thank the staff at North Light Books, and especially my editor, Jennifer Long, without whose help and suggestions I would have been overwhelmed.

Other fine North Light Books are available from your local bookstore or direct from the publisher.

03   02   01   00   99   5   4   3   2   1

Library of Congress Cataloging-in-Publication Data

Russell, Bill.
    Decorative furniture finishes with vinegar paint / by Bill Russell.
        p.   cm.
    Includes index.
    ISBN 0-89134-870-0 (pbk.: alk. paper)
    1. Furniture painting. 2. Finishes and finishing. 3. Decoration and ornament. I. Title.
TT199.4.R87   1999   98-41274
                                                          CIP

Editor: Jennifer Long
Production editor: Marilyn Daiker
Production coordinator: Erin Boggs
Designer: Brian Roeth

This book is dedicated to my family—in particular, my wonderful wife Mary, whose assistance has been invaluable and whose support and faith have been unstinting—and to my two extraordinary sons, Miles and Ian, who have brought so much joy to my life.

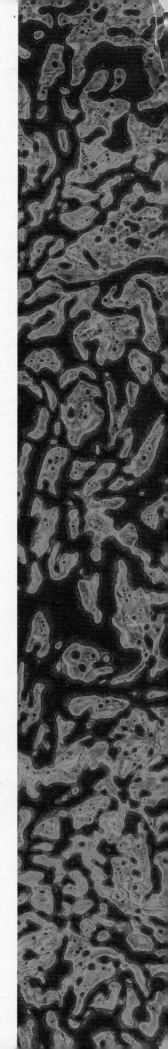

TABLE OF CONTENTS

PART ONE

Materials and Techniques

Learn all the basics of vinegar painting, from setting up your work station and choosing the best materials, to mixing up your own vinegar paint—use Bill's proven recipes to create a variety of colors and color combinations. Then follow along with seven step-by-step demonstrations to learn how to create unique vinegar paint textures, including:

1 *Burled Wood*
2 *Rolling Furrows*
3 *Quilted Wood*
4 *Fan Arcs*
5 *Plastic Wrap Pleats*
6 *Tiger Maple*
7 *Exotic Veneer*

PART TWO

Working With Furniture

Starting with a brief history of painted furniture, Bill teaches you how to select the right piece of furniture for a vinegar painting project, how to prepare the piece for painting and what aspects to consider when choosing color, pattern and additional decoration for your piece.

INTRODUCTION

What Is Paint?

The literature of painting contains countless recipes for paints that have particular color qualities, handling characteristics and degrees of permanence. But all paints share certain qualities: They are at some point liquid (this liquid part is known as the *vehicle*), they contain a coloring agent called *pigment* and they must have a *binder* to hold the pigment together once the vehicle has dried. Without the binder, the pigment will not stick to the surface onto which it has been painted.

The nature of any paint is determined by the various chemical and physical aspects of the vehicle, pigment and binder. The vehicle may be a naturally occurring material, such as beeswax or milk, or a highly sophisticated modern ingredient, such as an alkyd. Pigments range from manufactured chemicals to those found in the earth, and exhibit, in addition to the obvious color variations, a range of handling and performance characteristics. Binding may occur naturally when the vehicle dries, such as with linseed oil, which forms the vehicle of traditional oil paints; however, in the case of water-based paints, a separate ingredient must be added to assist in binding the particles of pigment after the water has evaporated. This additional binder may be some type of glue or, in the case of watercolor, a vegetable gum.

How Is Vinegar Paint Different?

Vinegar painting is a variation of a traditional decorative painting or faux painting technique, in which a thin layer of color is applied and manipulated over a dried basecoat of paint. In this technique, the vehicle of the decorative paint is an acidic liquid. Early recipes often cite stale beer for this ingredient, perhaps because it was more readily available than vinegar. Sugar in the beer or apple cider vinegar acts as the binder, allowing the particles of pigment to stay put after the vehicle has dried. (Anyone who has cleaned up a spilled beer or other sugary drink after it has dried can attest to sugar's binding property.) Moreover, the acidic nature of the liquid helps to clean the surface on which the mixture is painted so the dried paint will have a better bond.

Of course, sugar's bond is not very permanent. This wouldn't be a big problem if we were going to frame the finished painting under glass. But vinegar paint has special qualities that make it useful for decorating functional objects. Therefore, to become permanent, a strong binder must be added after it has dried. Traditionally, this extra binder was one or more coats of some type of clear varnish.

Some recipes for vinegar paint include other ingredients to alter the handling characteristics of the basic mixture; soap is a common addition. The soap helps to break down the surface tension of the base color and prevent cissing or beading of the vinegar paint. Therefore, vinegar paint is the mixture of apple cider vinegar, dry pigment and soap—this mixture meets the requirements for what we call paint.

The origins of this type of paint have been lost over time, but examples of it have been found from several centuries ago. The technique probably arrived on U.S. shores via craftsmen from the British Isles, who may have learned it from Swedish decorative artists. In any event, the use of vinegar paint was well established in this country by the early nineteenth century, as one may see by examining the surviving furniture of this period. Many of these pieces were finished with some type of paint, either in a solid color or in a more complex decorative technique.

Wardrobe, Louisville, Ohio, painted and grained poplar, 78" high × 60" wide × 20" deep (2m × 1.5m × 50.8cm), from the Collections of the Henry Ford Museum and Greenfield Village.

This early nineteenth-century grain-painted cupboard from Louisville, Ohio—an old French settlement—is a great example of exuberant glazing. While oil glazes were probably used, the variety of textures and directional strokes could also be accomplished with vinegar paint. More examples are shown on page 36.

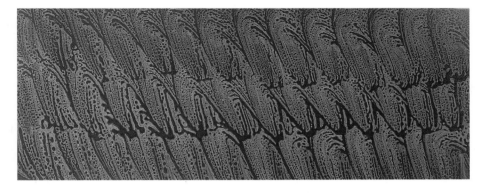

When the vinegar paint is brushed on freely, a variety of fanciful effects are possible.

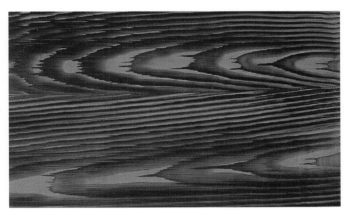

Vinegar paint can be used to create a convincing faux wood grain.

What Are the Advantages of Vinegar Paint?

One obvious question in considering this type of paint is, "What advantages would such a mixture have over more permanent paints?" The answer is that no other medium allows the artist to create the range of visual effects that can be achieved with this rather humble mixture.

Vinegar paint also has handling characteristics that give it great appeal. One advantage of the technique is its quickness in both the creation of the patterning and the drying of the paint. Moreover, it is easily reversed and can be removed and redone until satisfactory results are achieved. For these reasons, vinegar painting is a non-threatening technique that is less daunting for the novice than decorative painting techniques that require long drying intervals and may leave the learner with permanent mistakes.

While vinegar painting has had an important role in the history of grain painting—a subdivision of "faux painting" in which the objective is to copy the pattern and color of very specific woods—the technique has a great advantage in that it also can be highly interpretive or fanciful. Therefore, there is no strict, predetermined notion of what the results should look like. In fact, students in my workshops often create their own individual patterns and textures which I have never seen before. One of these students was a second grader at my sons' elementary school! And speaking of young students, since

no flammable solvents are used in the paint and the technique is reversible, with proper adult supervision it is appropriate for all ages.

Where Can You Make the Best Use of This Technique?

This brings us to the point of discovering where the patterns and textures created with vinegar paint can best be utilized. As mentioned earlier, both its visual and handling qualities make vinegar paint most appropriate for use in the decorative arts—for the ornamentation of useful things. Throughout history, the painting of utilitarian objects has had a twofold purpose: to preserve and to beautify the object. Beautification can be achieved by simply adding color or, more elaborately, by making the object look as though it were made of some exotic material. And herein lies another attraction of the vinegar paint technique: while protecting the surface through the application of the base and binder coats, one can add a variety of colorful effects, suggesting a wide range of materials.

But what type of surface or object would be best for this material? If you were to mix up some vinegar paint you would see that it would not be very useful for painting walls. If it's mixed thickly enough to stay on the wall, it would crack and quite possibly fall off when it dries. On the other hand, if it was mixed too thinly, it wouldn't cover very well and would run down the wall. Therefore, vinegar paint is best used on horizontal surfaces.

Additionally, since the mixture is most effective when mixed rather thinly, it doesn't work very well on undulating or textural surfaces, as the paint tends to collect in the low parts of the surface. For best results, seek out or create surfaces that are horizontal and smooth, such as those found on furniture, floors, boxes, interior accessories and some elements of woodwork, or surfaces that can be laid horizontal while you work, such as doors and other portable architectural elements. On these surfaces, a thin application of paint, which is best for texturing, will not run and will retain the imparted texture until it dries.

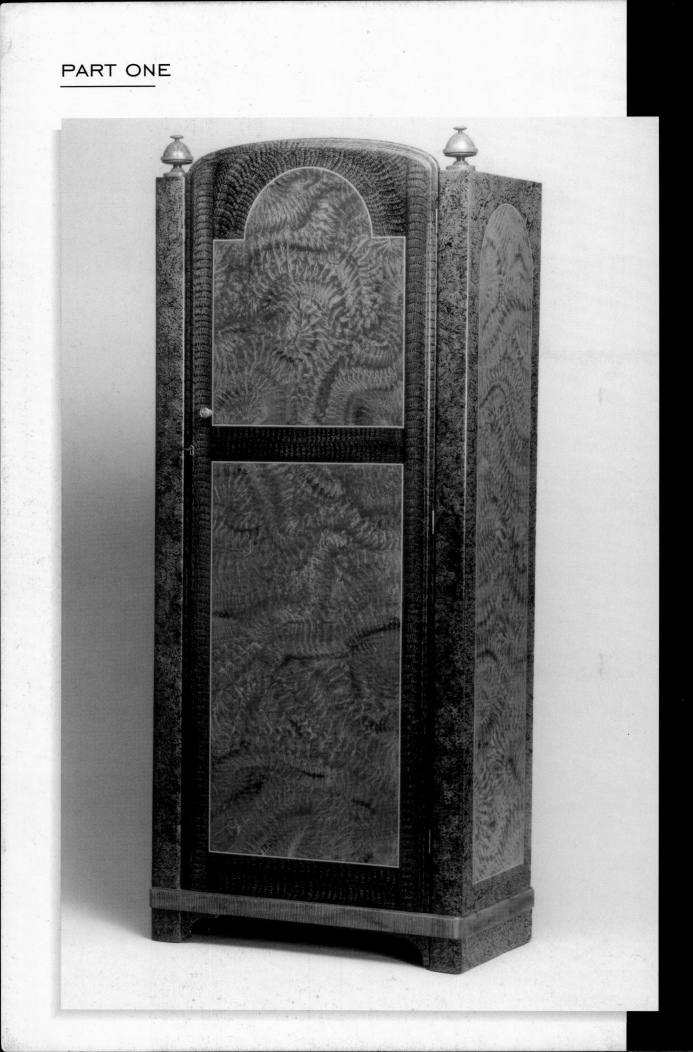

PART ONE

Materials and Techniques

In this chapter, we will explore the actual execution of the vinegar paint process. It is important that you attend to preparation so you are able to move smoothly through the process with success and satisfaction. What follows are suggestions based on my years of experimentation and application, but you should feel free to adapt my findings to your own situation and needs. Be alert to the "happy accident" that will allow you to develop your own color or textural result. Try to keep good records of base colors, pigments, texturing tools, etc. so you can reproduce an effect you like. But most importantly, have fun and take delight in your work. If things start off a bit unorganized and chaotic, hang in there. After you get a feel for how to work with the materials, some of the logistics will come naturally.

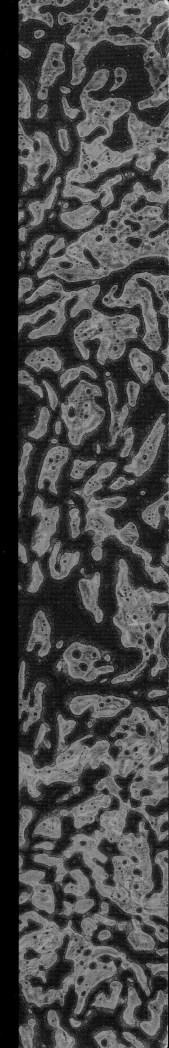

Armoire, 72" tall× 30" wide× 14" deep (1.8m× 76.2cm× 35.6cm), private collection.

SETTING UP A WORK STATION

In order to work effectively, you must first prepare your work area. By establishing a good environment, your work will be more enjoyable and will progress more quickly. Setting up an appropriate work space can usually be done inexpensively and without undue intrusion into your current environment. I have listed below some concerns that you should try to address.

Cleanliness

Cleanliness is important. Avoid areas that are dusty or that have debris drifting down from above. If you do your preparatory work, such as sanding, in the same space as your painting, be sure to sweep or vacuum thoroughly before you begin to paint. You may be able to protect your work from falling or settling debris by creating a sheltered area with plastic sheeting. Dust control is especially important when you varnish.

Lighting

Lighting should be strong enough and cover a wide enough area to enable you to see colors and details clearly. For small projects, a fluorescent, flexible-arm study lamp may suffice; for larger areas, consider hanging fluorescent shop lights. You don't need to worry too much about the type of lighting you choose making your colors appear different (your eyes will adjust), but keep in mind that fluorescent light will make colors look greener, while incandescent light will make colors look redder. Regular incandescent lighting is fine, but if it is from only a single source, you may find the shadows and highlights disturbing.

A combination of larger and smaller tables on wheels allows for the most flexible studio work station. An adjustable work light augments general studio lighting.

Storing pigments and paints on shelves allows for easy access. An auxiliary work counter is a good place to experiment and take notes.

Ventilation

Ventilation of your work area is especially important when you varnish, or if you choose to use oil-based colors. Since vinegar paint contains no solvents, it emits no fumes or vapors aside from the odor of the vinegar. However, oil paint and varnish contain volatile organic compounds that should not be inhaled. When using these materials, work in a well-ventilated indoor area. Ventilation means that you have both a fresh air source and an exhaust fan. While you may be tempted to try working outdoors, the presence of dirt, wind, sun and insects will have a negative effect on your results.

Workbench

You will need a table or workbench on which to mix, experiment with and apply the paint. I have found that one large and one or more small tables work best for me. The large table can be made by laying a piece of plywood across a couple of sawhorses. Of course, an old kitchen table or a desk will work just as well. Small tables, which will hold your pigments, brushes and samples as you work, can be fashioned from crates or cast-off furniture. I prefer my small tables to be lightweight or on casters so I can move them around the large table as I work. Small tables can double as supports while varnishing small doors or drawers, and if they have casters, you can turn the piece while applying the varnish, instead of walking around it. Shelves for storing your supplies and finished samples are helpful to keep materials from piling up on your worktable.

Drying Area

A drying area away from your worktable is a necessity. When you are painting furniture that has doors or drawers, these parts will need to be left to dry as you work on other parts. For small pieces a shelf may suffice, but for larger items a second set of sawhorses or another table would work better. Keep in mind that paints and varnish may take several hours to dry. Overhead hooks are also handy; some items may be hung up to clear surface areas.

Water

Access to water is very helpful. If no running water is available, supply yourself with a few small buckets of water to wash brushes and wipe up spills.

THE LAYERED LOOK

The basic technique used in applying vinegar paint is the layering of color, also commonly called glazing. This is one of the time-honored techniques of the great masters of western art. When light passes through a translucent film of color and bounces back to the eye, it has a different quality, a luminosity, that is not present when light is reflected from an opaque surface. This effect is used by the faux painter to imitate the subtle visual depth of stone, wood and other natural materials. When planning to use vinegar painting, you should always consider two important factors: It has to be applied in a translucent layer, and it has to be painted over a thoroughly dried base color, which will reflect a certain part of the visible spectrum of light back through the vinegar paint.

When vinegar paint is manipulated to create the chosen texture, the pigment will be pushed together in some areas and pulled away from other areas, resulting in different degrees of translucency and opacity. You will see more of the base color in areas where the pigment is pushed away, more of the pigment color in areas where the pigment is pushed together and a glaze-like combination of the colors in areas where a thin layer of pigment covers the base color. For instance, Prussian Blue vinegar paint applied over an ochre base color will result in a deep blue color where the pigment is piled up, ochre where the pigment is removed or pushed apart, and medium green where a thin layer of pigment covers the base color. While all of this may sound very complex, it actually happens automatically when you apply the vinegar paint and texture it with one of the various manipulative techniques shown on the sample boards in part two.

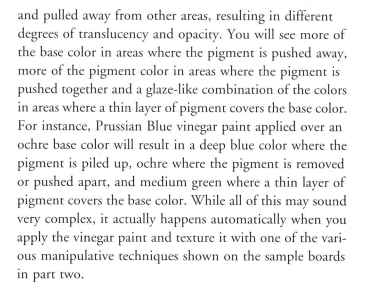

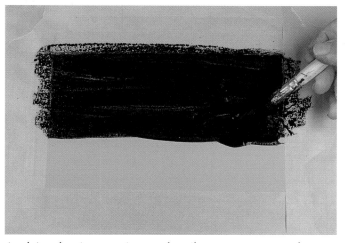

Applying the vinegar paint very heavily creates an opaque layer—deep blue in this case.

Brushing the paint out more thinly creates an overall glaze or combination of the two colors. Notice how the thin areas have taken on a green appearance.

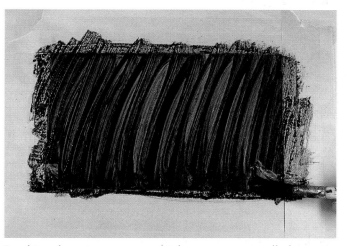

Texturing the paint by pressing into it with the brush forces the paint into thick and thin areas and also reveals the base color in some places, creating three distinct color effects—blue, green and ochre.

SURFACES, PRIMERS AND BASE PAINTS

The application and texturing of the vinegar paint over the dried base color form the meat of the vinegar paint technique sandwich. The primer is the bottom piece of bread and the varnish is the top piece. One of the most important things to keep in mind about this process is that, unlike most painting processes, how you apply the vinegar paint is less important than what you do to it once it is applied. Because texturing or patterning is done by moving or removing some of the paint, it is commonly referred to as a "removal process."

In the fine arts, a picture is usually painted by applying paint with brushes to build up an image, stroke by stroke. In most of the vinegar paint techniques, there is no "stroke by stroke." The paint is brushed on rapidly and freely to completely cover a section of the surface. Then the image (texture) is created by moving and/or taking away some of the paint. Your choice of texturing tool and manipulation technique will provide specific visual results. (See the sample boards later in this part to learn how various textures and patterns are created.)

Vinegar paint is always applied over a dried base paint, and the base paint should always be applied over a good primer. The primer should be applied to a smooth, clean surface, whether it be paper, cardboard, wood or metal. You can use oil- or water-based primers and base paints— it's purely a matter of personal choice. I prefer water-based primers for most work. However, if you are working over metal, laminate or some other non-wood material, oil-based primer may be more compatible. Check with your local paint dealer for the most appropriate primer.

Alkyd Paint

Your choice of basecoat could be based on a variety of factors. If you want to use traditional methods, take your cue from nineteenth-century artisans, who used a linseed oil paint for their base color.

The modern equivalent of linseed oil paint is called *alkyd*, which derives its name phonetically from two of its chemical parents: *alc*ohol and ac*id*. This material has similar handling characteristics to linseed oil paints and is thinned with chemical solvents. When you go to a paint store and ask for oil paint, you are actually getting alkyd paint. (This applies to housepaint only, not to artist-quality oil or alkyd paints.)

Alkyd paint makes a wonderful base for vinegar painting, because it brushes out to a very smooth finish. Also, because it is non-porous, it tends to absorb neither the pigment nor the liquid from the vinegar paint. This means the base color will retain its true color and the vinegar paint will dry relatively slowly, allowing a little more time for textural manipulation.

The drawbacks of alkyd paints are that they can be messy to work with, can require a relatively long drying time and can require the use of volatile, flammable liquids for thinning and clean-up.

Latex Paint

An alternative material to alkyd paint is latex paint. Just as today's "oil" housepaints probably don't contain any oil, "latex" paints may not contain any latex. *Emulsion*—the name by which latex paints are known outside the U.S.— is a more appropriate name for this type of paint because of its unique chemical composition. It is important to know that the better latex paints today are actually acrylic emulsions.

Latex paint has some disadvantages compared to alkyd paint (oil), but it can also serve very nicely as the basecoat for vinegar paint. On the negative side, since latex paints are porous, some brands may tend to stain when they absorb the pigment in the vinegar paint. However, the better-performing brands will do so only minimally, if at all.

This porosity may also allow some of the liquid from the vinegar paint to soak into the base paint, causing the surface to dry more quickly (cutting down on the time you have to manipulate the texture) than if you were using an alkyd base. But again, this would only be a noticeable factor with certain brands of paint or under very dry operating conditions.

Finally, latex paint tends to retain brush marks more noticeably than oil paint, but this characteristic can be minimized, if not entirely eliminated, by thinning the paint slightly when you apply it and sanding with the appropriate sandpaper between coats.

On the positive side, latex paints are pleasant to work with since they require only water for thinning and clean-up. More importantly, their lack of flammable solvents not only makes them less dangerous to use but also means they pose less of a health risk. They also dry more quickly to the touch, allowing objects to be handled, recoated or vinegar painted sooner than oil-painted objects. For most people, latex base paint is the better choice.

Ultimately, whether you choose to work with alkyd or latex paint depends upon your personal preference and upon having the appropriate work space. For some individuals, health concerns may also be a determining factor, since the solvents in alkyd paints present safety issues.

VINEGAR PAINT FORMULATION

As previously mentioned, vinegar paint is a mixture of *apple cider vinegar*, soap or detergent, and pigment. Apple cider vinegar is readily available at most grocery stores. Dry pigments may be purchased from better art supply stores or mail ordered (see the appendix, pages 126-127). The soap I use is liquid dish detergent, and while I prefer a non-colored, non-perfumed type, any brand is okay. I premix a container of the liquid medium in a plastic squeeze bottle, which I can then combine with different pigments to create the colors that I wish to work with.

To make the liquid medium:

1 Add ⅛ teaspoon (0.6ml) of dish detergent to 1 pint (0.5l) of vinegar. You may need a little more or less soap, depending on the concentration of your brand. Too much soap will cause the vinegar paint to suds up and become bubbly; if there is too little soap, the vinegar paint will not hold the texture very well, or it may bead up on the surface.

To make the paint:

2 Put a small amount, 1 teaspoon (5ml) or less, of the dry pigment into a wide-mouth container—I use an empty tuna can or half-pint (0.25l) plastic deli container.

3 Add the premixed liquid medium (vinegar plus soap) to the pigment. The amount of medium you need will vary with the different pigments, and you will have to add more medium periodically due to evaporation. Too little vinegar medium will result in a thick opaque paint, and too much medium will make a runny mixture that will not hold a texture.

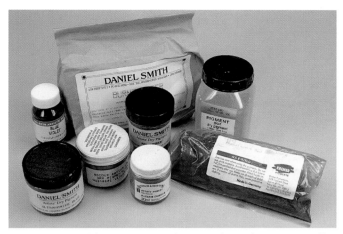

Pigments are sold in various packages and weights. Buy small quantities until you have established your preferences.

4 The pigment and vinegar medium must be stirred vigorously with the no. 2 oval sash brush until well mixed. A few small bubbles may appear from the soap, but the mixture should not become foamy.

Think of mixing the vinegar paint as though you were whipping a small amount of cream. For this reason, it is best if you work with small amounts of the paint. I usually start out with about a half teaspoon (2.5ml) of pigment and mix more paint as I need it. While it is possible to mix a larger quantity and store it in an airtight container, you must always be sure that the pigment is totally stirred or shaken into the medium before use, or it will settle out to the bottom of the container.

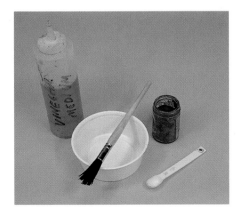

Mix the vinegar paint in a shallow container such as a plastic deli dish. Use a measuring spoon to maintain the correct proportion of pigment to vinegar.

Put the pigment into the dish first. Then, still using the measuring spoon, add the vinegar/soap mixture.

Stir vigorously and thoroughly to combine the ingredients until small bubbles appear in the paint. Repeat this stirring process before every application of the paint, or the pigment will settle to the bottom of the container.

COLOR RECIPES

With some experience, you can mix the pigment and medium without measuring, but in the beginning it is best to follow the recipes, since the various pigments have different mixing characteristics. When applied to the base color, the vinegar paint should be thick enough to maintain some brushstrokes, but not so thick that it obscures the base color completely. Since the pigments have various chemical and physical properties, they will behave differently from one another in the vinegar medium. Some will mix easily with the medium, while others will require a good stirring. Following are some notes on the pigments I use most.

While there are many other pigments available, these will give you a wide variety of color effects and have proven to be dependable performers. You could begin with the earth tones and expand your palette from there. If you wish to try colors not on the chart, by all means do so. You may find a particular color quality you are seeking. Experiment with other pigments to widen your experience with color and pigment characteristics.

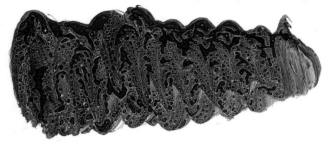

Burnt Umber
1 part pigment to 2 parts vinegar medium. Rich brown color, easy to work, a good dark wood tone over ochre base.

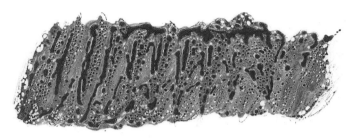

Burnt Sienna
1 part pigment to 2 parts vinegar medium. Reddish brown color, easy to work, gives a cherry or red maple tone over ochre base.

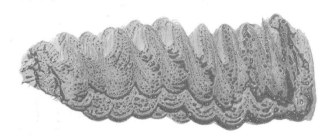

Raw Sienna
1 part pigment to 2 parts vinegar medium. Rich tan color, easy to work, especially good for modifying other earth tones.

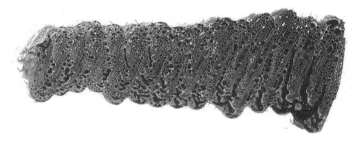

Indian Red (Mars Red)
1 part pigment to 2 parts vinegar medium. Rust color, easy to work, gives a rich mahogany tone over ochre.

Cadmium Red Light
1 part pigment to 2 parts vinegar medium. Bright reddish orange, easy to work, interesting when mixed wet-in-wet with Manganese Violet.

Cadmium Red Medium
1 part pigment to 3 parts vinegar medium. Strong red color, may require a little extra soap to hold the desired texture. Try adding a small amount of an earth tone to improve handling.

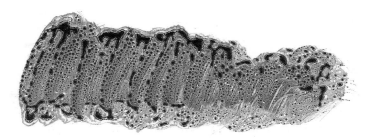

Transparent Red (Kremer #5240)
1 part pigment to 4 parts vinegar medium. Gives a beautiful coppery tone when sufficiently thinned; otherwise, tends to be murky.

Alizarin Crimson Lake (Imitation Rose Madder)
1 part pigment to 4 parts vinegar medium. Beautiful deep-red color. Handles better than Alizarin Crimson, which tends to be gritty.

Manganese Violet
2 parts pigment to 3 parts vinegar medium. Beautiful light violet. Handles well when mixed properly; otherwise, tends to be weak. Looks powdery and opaque when dry but turns transparent and bold when varnished.

Prussian (Milori) Blue
1 part pigment to 4 parts vinegar medium. Very strong deep blue. Works well when thin; otherwise, overpowers base color. Good for dropping into or blending with other pigments for wet-in-wet technique.

Cobalt Blue
1 part pigment to 2 parts vinegar medium. Rich medium blue. Handles better than most other blues, which can be hard to control. Blends well with other pigments.

Viridian Green
1 part pigment to 2 parts vinegar medium. Slightly bluish green, handles well but tends to dry very quickly. Mix with black for a rich, dark, antique green.

Mars Black
1 part pigment to 2 parts vinegar medium. Handles well; good for modifying other pigments. Can be used by itself over very light or bright pigments.

Titanium White
1 part pigment to 4 parts vinegar medium. Opaque—as are all whites. Tends to leave a filmy haze over base colors, but can be effective where a "pickled" look is desired or can be used to modify other pigments. Will impart opaqueness to any pigment it is mixed with.

PREPARING A SAMPLE BOARD

The following sample boards show some of the textures I commonly use. The complete preparation process is illustrated on these two pages. The other examples show only the technique used to create the texture, but they require the same preparation of the surface as shown here.

MATERIALS FOR SAMPLE BOARDS

• **Coated railroad**—This relatively lightweight cardboard has a clay coating on one side that makes it slightly shiny and prevents paint from soaking in. It is usually available from art supply stores that cater to sign painters. You can use regular lightweight cardboard for samples; but you may find that if you use latex paint it will soak in and cause the board to buckle. To prevent this, use an oil primer or base paint.

• **Drafting tape**—This is available at good art supply stores, especially those that stock materials for architects. *Beware of masking tape.* It is too sticky and will tear up the board when you try to remove it.

• **A good-quality 1-inch to 2-inch (2.5cm to 5.1cm) paint brush**—Natural bristles work better for oil paints, and nylon bristles work better for latex paints.

• **Primer**—Latex universal primers work well. I use Zinsser Bulls Eye 1 2 3 brand. Your local paint store will have a similar product. If you are painting uncoated cardboard, you will need to use an oil primer to prevent the board from buckling. One quart will prime many boards. You can have the primer tinted at the paint store to match your base color.

• **High-quality latex or oil-based interior enamel**—I generally prefer latex paint with an "eggshell" or "low luster" sheen. On these sample boards, I used Muralo Ultra Eggshell. This latex paint performs very nicely and compares to oil enamel. The traditional straw color I used is called Pigskin—other paint manufacturers will have different names for this color. A slight variation in the base color will not have much effect on your final result.

• **A no. 2 natural-bristle oval sash brush**—*Nylon bristle brushes will not work well with the vinegar paint.* The no. 2 oval sash brush is used for mixing, applying and, in some cases, texturing the vinegar paint. Better hardware stores or home supply centers carry these inexpensive brushes. Buy several so you can keep one for each color of pigment.

• **Burnt Umber vinegar paint**—Mix the paint as follows: in a tuna can or deli container, combine 2 parts vinegar medium to 1 part Burnt Umber dry pigment. I use kitchen measuring spoons for this purpose. You may have to vary this recipe for different weather conditions or to create certain textures. Also, since the mixture is constantly drying out due to the vinegar evaporation, you will have to add more vinegar medium periodically.

• **Gloss or semi-gloss polyurethane or traditional oil-based varnish**—*Avoid water-based varnish or shellac.* The vinegar paint will smear if you try to coat it with one of these products.

• **A small 1-inch or 1½-inch (2.5cm to 3.8cm) high-quality natural-bristle varnish brush**

• **Mineral spirits**—This will remove oil paint and varnish from your brushes.

• **Sandpaper**—You will need 150-grit sandpaper for removing brush marks in the primer or first basecoat, and 220-grit sandpaper for sanding out brush marks and dust from the final basecoat. Special sandpaper for latex is expensive, but it will do a better job because it is less likely to clog up with the paint particles (see appendix, pages 126-127).

• **Texturing tools**—As shown in the following samples.

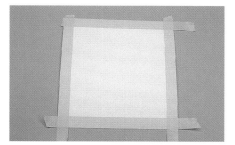  

1 Cut an 8″ (20.3cm) square of coated railroad board and tape it down with drafting tape. The coated side will be slightly shiny.

2 Prime the surface with a good-quality water-based or oil-based primer and let dry. Be sure to use oil-based primer if the cardboard is uncoated.

3 Sand lightly with 150-grit (medium) or 220-grit (fine) sandpaper and wipe off dust.

4 Brush on a coat of base color, oil or latex, and let dry. Sand again with 150-grit sandpaper if the surface is still fairly rough, or use 220-grit sandpaper if the surface appears smooth. Wipe clean.

5 Apply a second coat of the base color and let dry.

6 Sand with 220-grit sandpaper and wipe. If you are doing a lot of samples, paint a whole board and cut it afterwards.

This completes the application of the base color and the preparation for the application of the vinegar paint. Up to this point, the preparation and application techniques have been the same for all texture/pattern samples. Now we will explore how various textures are achieved. These basic textures can be combined or modified to result in a grand array of textural possibilities.

Sample Board 1
BURLED WOOD

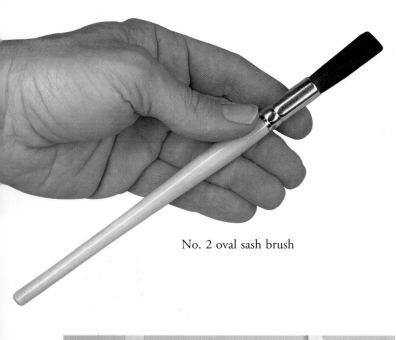

No. 2 oval sash brush

1 With the no. 2 oval sash brush, brush on a coat of the vinegar paint at the proper consistency. You may have to scrub the paint onto the surface to keep the paint from cissing or beading up. This is especially likely if you are using oil paint for your base color.

2 Notice the brush marks of the vinegar paint are visible, but there is paint over the entire surface. If the paint is too thick, you will not be able to see the base color. If it is too thin, the base color will be too obvious.

3 After coating the board with the vinegar paint and while it is still wet, use the same no. 2 oval sash brush to vigorously stipple the surface. Use a quick vertical motion and really push the brush into the surface. Lift the brush off the surface and rotate it slightly between each stipple. Work quickly around the board in a random pattern, making sure you hit all parts of the surface.

4 The paint may continue to crawl a bit after you finish working, but this will only add to the desired effect of randomness. If you continue to work after the paint begins to dry, the effect will be lost and the result will be smudgy. The finished board should resemble the random directional pattern of a burled wood.

5 Working in one direction, apply an even coat of varnish and let dry (see part four for more finishing information). A second coat of varnish is good insurance, even on a sample board.

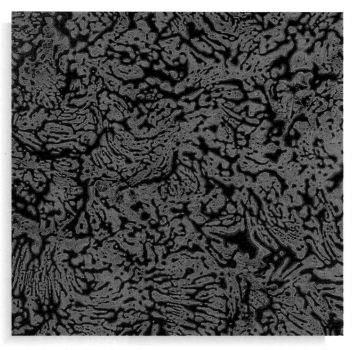

6 After the varnish is dry, remove the tape to observe the finished sample.

TIPS

• If the results are not satisfactory, try again. You can wipe off the first attempt with a damp rag and start over, or use a spray bottle filled with vinegar medium and reconstitute the dried paint by spraying and brushing it with the same brush used for application. This should allow you to redistribute and retexture the vinegar paint.

• If you use latex paint for the base, be careful not to work over it too long, or the vinegar will begin to dissolve the latex. Depending on the brand of latex paint and the amount of time you let it dry, you should have several minutes before this will happen.

• After it has dried, the vinegar paint will have lost its gloss and will look rather lifeless. Don't panic! It will return to its beautiful appearance (or look even better) when you apply the varnish.

ROLLING FURROWS

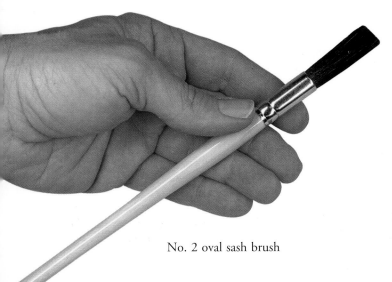

No. 2 oval sash brush

1 Brush on the vinegar paint with a no. 2 sash brush.

2 Lay the sash brush on its side and roll it through the paint in a series of straight lines.

3 When you finish, these rows will cover the entire surface and will resemble the furrows of a plowed field.

4 Varnish the surface and remove the tape for the finished effect.

Sample Board 3
QUILTED WOOD

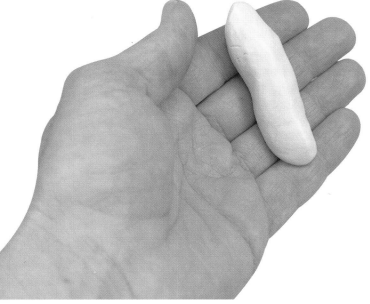

1 Form a small lump of putty or glazing compound into a finger shape.

2 Brush on the vinegar paint with a no. 2 oval sash brush.

3 As soon as the board is covered, grasp the piece of putty and stamp it into the vinegar paint in rows.

4 Continue this process until the board is covered. This pattern will resemble the quilted pattern of certain woods, such as sapele. If the paint dries before you finish, repaint the surface and try again, this time working faster.

5 Varnish the board and, when dry, remove the tape for the finished sample.

For a serpentine variation, move the putty in a random series of arcs or curves.

Sample Board 4
FAN ARCS

Large no. 10 or no. 12 natural-bristle fan brush

1 Brush on the vinegar paint with a no. 2 oval sash brush.

2 Lay a large no. 10 or no. 12 fan brush nearly horizontal and press it into the vinegar paint so that the tip of the brush leaves an arc in the paint. Repeat this process to create a row of arcs with approximately ¼" (.6cm) between arcs.

3 Continue until there are enough rows of arcs to cover the board.

4 Varnish the board and, when dry, remove the tape for the finished sample.

PLEATS

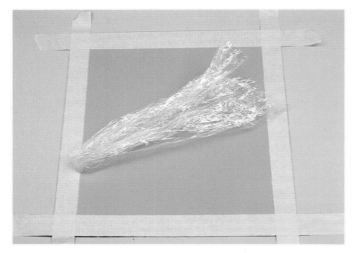

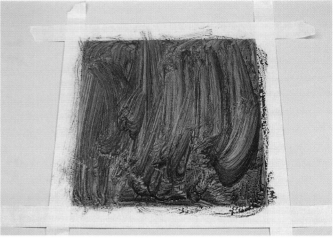

1 Pull off approximately one square foot (30cm²) of plastic food wrap. Gather the plastic wrap into a rope-like configuration and fold this shape in half to create a series of pleats.

2 Brush on the vinegar paint with a no. 2 oval sash brush.

3 Grasp both ends of the plastic wrap. While stretching it tight, stamp it through the vinegar paint.

4 Repeat as often as needed to cover the board.

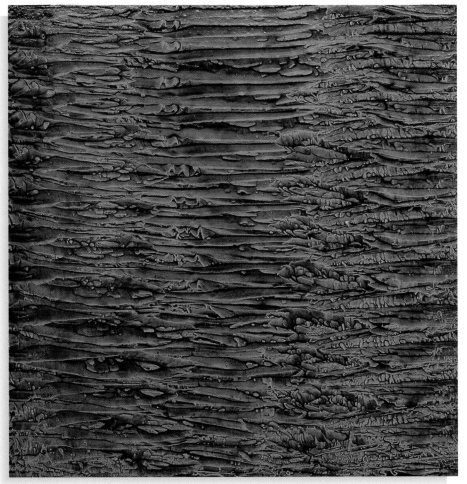

5 Varnish the board and, when dry, remove the tape for the finished sample.

Sample Board 6
TIGER MAPLE

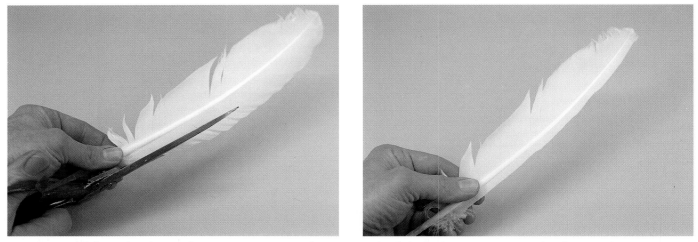

1 Select a well-formed turkey quill. Use scissors to trim the convex side of the feather to approximately ¼″ (.6cm) long.

2 After brushing on the vinegar paint, use the quill to briskly strike the surface of the wet paint along the length of the board. This will create a series of very closely spaced lines.

3 Continue this process on the remainder of the board so that the lines cover the entire surface.

4 Varnish the board and, when dry, remove the tape for the finished sample. The resulting pattern will resemble tiger maple.

Sample Board 7
EXOTIC VENEER

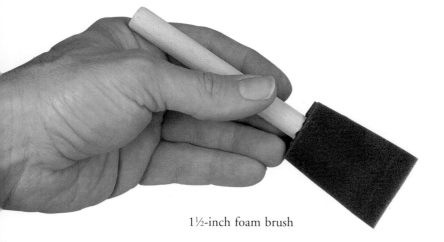

1½-inch foam brush

1 After brushing on the vinegar paint, walk the foam brush through the paint by alternately pivoting the corners forward. (The series of motions is similar to the method you would use to move a refrigerator by yourself.) Your pattern may vary from mine, but you should strive for regularity.

2 Continue this process in rows to cover the board.

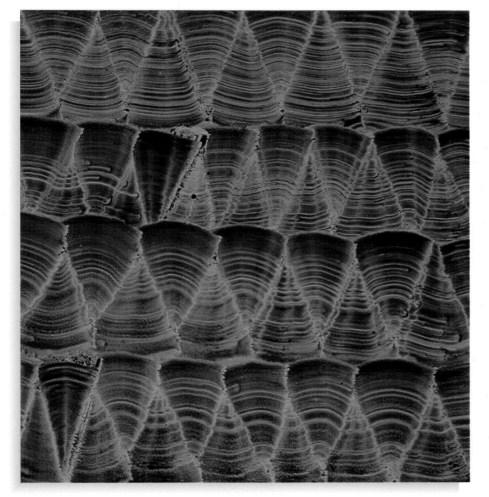

3 Varnish the board and, when dry, remove the tape for the finished sample. This is a very optical pattern and suggests the visual effect of an exotic veneer.

COLOR COMBINATIONS

Pigments may be used to create different color effects in three ways:

• Individual pigments mixed with vinegar medium will create strong, identifiable colors.

• Combinations of different pigments mixed with the medium will create a greater range of color with more subtlety.

• Premixed vinegar paints of different colors may be combined on the surface in a wet-in-wet technique to create an organic color variety, as found in wood or stone.

If you want to change from one color or texture to another in a gradual transition, change or add pigment as you go. To gradually blend two colors wet-in-wet, follow the demonstration below.

Abrupt changes in color or texture are difficult, since the texturing is rather bold and requires a free range of motion. If you don't want to blend colors, you will have to create borders between different areas. Taping is the most efficient method for doing this (see page 41).

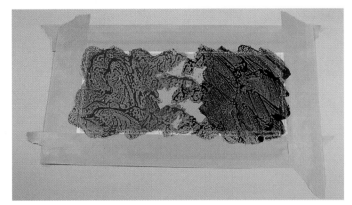

1 To create a blended color, apply different colors at opposite ends of the area you wish to paint. For a dramatic effect, try Manganese Violet and Prussian Blue on an ochre base color.

2 Use the no. 2 sash brush to begin mixing the colors together where they meet. Continue until the color change appears gradual but remains limited to the center section of the panel.

3 Use a feather or other texturing tool to work across the panel in one direction. This will continue the blending process.

4 If necessary, you may repeat the texturing process a second or third time to make the blending more subtle.

5 The effect will be most apparent when the varnish is applied.

BINDING, PRESERVING AND VARNISHING

After the vinegar paint dries, it will look very dull and lifeless. But fear not! The wonderful colors that were apparent when the surface was wet will return when you apply the final finish. You will get used to this dramatic change after you work on a few sample boards. It is even possible to preview the final appearance by taking a soft brush, such as a flat artist's watercolor brush, and applying mineral spirits or naphtha to a small part of the surface of the dried vinegar paint. When you do this, the color will come up to closely resemble the finished surface. Remember that the binder (sugar) is water soluble, so don't try this with water or you will disturb the texture you have just created. This effect will only last a moment or two until the solvent evaporates, but it will be long enough for you to see if you have achieved the desired result.

When you have finished vinegar-painting an area, it is time to apply the finish, which will bind the paint and protect the surface. Your finishing options are as follows:
- Traditional solvent-based (alkyd) varnish
- Solvent-based polyurethane varnish
- Lacquer

Alkyd and polyurethane varnish have similar handling characteristics. Lacquer, a very different type of finish, requires special solvents and handling. These materials and their application techniques are discussed in detail in part four.

Water-based finishes and shellac are *not* recommended and are not compatible with vinegar paint. The water-based finishes will break down the sugar binder and destroy the texture or patterning that has been achieved. Shellac, because it contains alcohol as a solvent, will tend to do the same thing, causing the vinegar paint to smear as the shellac is brushed over it. While these materials have their advantages for other finishing applications, they are not appropriate protective coatings for vinegar paint.

A SAFETY NOTE

It is important to understand that, while the materials of the vinegar paint technique are not inherently dangerous, all non-edible substances are potential health hazards if mishandled, ingested or inhaled. Even vinegar, a

food product which is mildly acidic, may cause skin irritation in some individuals.

Plastic gloves and an approved respirator are recommended safety equipment for handling powdered pigments. Pigments containing metals such as cobalt, cadmium, manganese and titanium are considered poisonous and should be treated accordingly.

The solvents in the finishes are volatile and may present a concern for both health and safety. However, by following the simple precautions listed on product labels and elsewhere in this book (see part one, "Setting Up A Work Station"), it is quite possible to work at home safely and without undue risk to your health.

It is very important to read and follow the directions for all art or finishing materials you purchase. When in doubt, it is better to err on the side of caution.

PART TWO

Working
With
Furniture

Who knows when the first Homo sapiens discovered it was more comfortable to pull a stone or piece of wood up to the fire than to sit on the cold ground. Whenever it was, that person invented furniture. Some time later, another of our ancestors found the "furniture" could be preserved if fat or oil was applied to it. Another enterprising individual personalized his furniture through the addition of color. Thus was born one branch of the decorative arts: furniture painting.

Drop-Front Desk, 36" wide× 18" deep× 45" tall (91.4cm× 45.7cm× 1.1m), collection of the artist

A HISTORY OF PAINTED FURNITURE

Furniture painting is not a recent development. Many museums contain collections of ancient painted furniture, such as that found in the tomb of the Egyptian king Tut-ankhamen which dates back to the second millennium B.C.E. In the U.S., there is a rich history of furniture painting, as can be seen by touring our museums and folk art collections, or reading books such as Dean Fales's *American Painted Furniture*.

Some of this painting is a simple coat of protective color, as in the case of Shaker furniture, and some of it is of fantastic design, as in the work of the Pennsylvania Germans. Some of the painting was done by the farmer who fashioned the stool he needed for his barn, and some was done by highly skilled and trained artists. Materials and techniques varied from the homemade and humble to the refined and intricate. But the relationship among color, texture, form and function has been and continues to be an exciting area of exploration.

Worktable, Massachusetts, from the collection of the Smithsonian Institution.

A combination of brown and green vinegar paint was used on this Hepplewhite-style worktable, painted between 1820 and 1830. Note the lack of variety or directional change in the patterning, suggesting that the work was done by an untrained artisan.

Schrank, Lancaster County, Pennsylvania, painted and grained pine, 88½" high × 88" wide × 23⅞" deep (2.25m × 2.2m × 606cm), from the Collections of the Henry Ford Museum and Greenfield Village.

This German-American wardrobe dates from the late seventeenth century. Paint is used in a variety of ways: to create the look of stone on the panels and drawers, for a mottled grain effect on the frame and for the striking, stylized floral motifs.

Chest, New England, from the collection of the Smithsonian Institution.

This small chest was vinegar painted between 1825 and 1840. Red, black and green were used over a yellow base. Linseed oil putty or leather would have been used to create the patterning.

CHOOSING THE RIGHT PIECE OF FURNITURE TO PAINT

If you would like to share in this rich tradition, you need only two things: a piece of furniture and painting materials. If you combine the right colors and design with just the right piece of furniture, you may end up with a decorative masterpiece.

Let's consider what characteristics you might want in that "right" piece of furniture. Age, style, size, condition, construction and material are all important factors in your selection.

CHECKLIST FOR CHOOSING AN OBJECT TO PAINT

1 Make sure the piece is not a bona-fide antique that would be devalued if painted.

2 Determine that the piece is structurally sound. Loose joints or missing parts could spell trouble down the road. A quick way to evaluate the general quality of a piece of furniture is to examine the drawers. Dovetail joints indicate better construction.

3 Examine the surface for serious damage or a cracked or peeling finish that would have to be completely stripped. This wouldn't disqualify a piece, but it would make it more time-consuming or expensive to paint.

4 Keep it simple. Too many doors, compartments, spindles and carved or applied surface decorations can make a project difficult.

5 Keep it small, especially in the beginning. Boxes, frames, small tables and stands are good choices.

6 Look for furniture that has a smooth, close-grained surface. Avoid open-grained woods, such as oak, in which the pores of the wood are very obvious. If you want to work on oak, it's important to fill the pores with a special grain-filling paste to make the surface smooth. This step may already be done in a previously finished oak piece.

7 Be sensitive to the inherent beauty of particular woods. Strive to paint only those objects that will look better when painted. If you were to paint over solid domestic hardwoods such as cherry or walnut, or over an imported hardwood such as mahogany, it is likely that someone at a future date would be tempted to return the furniture to its "original" state. Of course, an exception can be made if a piece has already been painted or has suffered damage that would make its natural appearance unappealing. Pine, poplar, maple, alder and other close-grained woods are suitable to paint, with the harder maple being very desirable. Wood identification can be difficult for a variety of reasons. If you are unsure about what wood your piece is made of, it may be worthwhile to consult a knowledgeable person before beginning.

8 Metal or laminate-covered objects can be painted if you follow the proper steps (see page 39).

Painting Over Veneer

Veneer is a very thin layer of expensive or exotic wood that has been glued to a less interesting or cheaper base wood. Most manufactured wooden furniture contains at least some veneer. Unless it is deeply gouged or allowed to absorb moisture, veneer is quite durable. However, when it gets wet, the glue holding it to the underlying wood may weaken. Loose veneer can often be identified by a bubble-like form on the surface. While it is possible to repair, this can be a time-consuming process. If most of the veneer has lifted from a surface, you may be tempted to try to remove it all by scraping or sanding. This usually results in an undesirable surface and may even affect the structural integrity of the furniture.

Therefore, examine any veneered piece of furniture to see that the veneer is adhered tightly to the surface. Besides looking for the telltale bubbles, you can do this by lightly tapping your fingernails on the surface. You will hear a ringing sound where the veneer is tight, and a slightly deeper, more hollow sound where the veneer is loose. If you detect loose veneer, look for another candidate for your project. However, if the veneer is sound and adhered tightly to the underlying wood, there is no reason it can't be painted. In fact, you will increase the durability of the veneer by painting it because it is very unlikely that any moisture will penetrate the paint and finish.

THE ARCHITECTURE OF FURNITURE

Furniture is constructed much like a building: some elements, such as legs and framing members, are structural or supportive; other elements, such as doors and drawers, are functional but not structural; and still others, such as finials and applied decoration, are purely decorative. Just as in a building, it is not unusual for these parts to exhibit different visual characteristics. The type of wood, direction of the grain or even the choice of whether to use metal or stone for part of the piece may all be influenced by its architecture. Therefore, when planning how to paint a piece of furniture, consider its architecture and use the parts that have different functions as a guide to changing color, texture and pattern direction.

When you want to combine two or more colors and/or textures on a piece of furniture, you will either have to gradually blend them wet-in-wet (see page 32), or you will have to end each texture or color to begin another. These abrupt transitions may be made by taping or masking off the areas from each other, or they may be made by taking advantage of physical breaks that occur in the piece. As you will see in the projects in part three, ⅛" (.3cm) automotive masking tape and ¾" (1.9cm) drafting tape are indispensable tools. When working with tape, you must be sure to burnish it by pressing down evenly along its length with your fingernail. If paint leaks under the tape, you may find that painting over the tape with a thin layer of the base color and letting it dry before adding vinegar paint will help you achieve a crisp edge.

Some styles of furniture have more of these physical breaks and are, therefore, more easily divided into different color/texture combinations. You will benefit from furniture that exhibits the following characteristics:

1 Square edges are easier to work with than rounded edges. "Waterfall" furniture, popular in the 1940s, has a rounded transition from top to front, no physical definition separates these parts. This doesn't mean it is unsuitable, but it does mean you will have to mask these parts off, paint and finish the top and then remove and reposition the tape on the front of the piece.

2 Legs of chests and stands which are raised from the sides and front of the piece will give you a natural place to change the texture or color and emphasize structure. Square legs are preferable to round legs, which have no flat surfaces and are difficult to texture, as the paint tends to run around the legs.

3 Drawers that are separated by a visible horizontal element or rail will have better definition than those that appear to simply sit on top of each other.

4 Overhanging tops provide a better opportunity to break up the pattern than tops that are flush with the sides.

5 Flat surfaces are almost always preferable to carved, textured or built-up surfaces.

6 A door that has a raised frame and panel construction, as opposed to a simple flat panel, will provide an added opportunity to vary the surface pattern.

Good Choices
The two pieces at left, though different in style, are good choices for vinegar painting because they have flat, simple surfaces, few parts and no elaborate decoration. The jelly cupboard, while relatively large at about four feet tall (1.2m), has a Shaker style that lends itself well to decorative finishing. Unlike the bedside table, it is a new piece of unpainted furniture. Similar pieces are available from unpainted furniture stores in most areas.

Poor Choices
The table and tea cart at left are less appropriate choices for vinegar painting because of the complex structure and detail. The shelves and leaves of the teacart and the elaborately turned legs of the table would be difficult to paint, so beginners should consider other choices.

PREPARATION FOR PAINTING

Once you have selected an object to paint, you will need to prepare it. If this is not done properly, your ability to do a good job of painting and finishing will be severely hampered. Depending on the age and condition of the piece, some or all of the following steps will need to be followed:

1 Disassembly
Remove all hardware, including knobs, hinges and handles.

2 Cleaning
Any dirt or debris should be brushed, scraped or washed off all surfaces of the piece. Be careful not to soak veneered surfaces with water while cleaning; however, it is fine to wipe the veneer with a damp cloth, followed by a dry cloth. Mineral spirits or naphtha may be helpful to dissolve some surface dirt—especially when used in concert with fine-grade steel wool—and these solvents will not affect the veneer glue. If, at this point, the surface appears to be in very bad condition, with a peeling or cracked finish, you may have to strip it chemically or consider using another object.

3 Repairing and Filling
Now you should make the necessary repairs. Reglue joints or other parts if needed. If this type of work is beyond your abilities, pick another project. Next, fill in any holes or gouges in the surface with patching compound. I use spackling paste for most small fills, but on corners or to build up large areas, a solvent-based patching material, such as Plastic Wood, or an epoxy putty is better. Holes may need to be sanded and refilled until flush with the surface. Be sure to sand away all extra patching material when dry, since you don't want any raised areas on the surface.

4 Sanding
Now the whole piece should be sanded to prepare the old finish for the primer. I use 120-grit sandpaper for rougher or badly aged surfaces and 150-grit sandpaper for those surfaces in good shape. It isn't necessary to remove all the old finish; you just want to sand away the part that is dirty or oxidized. If the piece is made of metal or laminate, the sanding process will also create a series of small scratches that will provide a "tooth" for the primer to grasp onto.

5 Final Wiping
After sanding, wipe the piece again with a cloth dampened with mineral spirits. This will remove residual wax and dirt that the sanding dislodged or left behind. These steps need to be followed with all the parts of the piece, such as doors and drawers. If you are working on new, unpainted furniture, it will only need to be sanded and wiped with a tack cloth or vacuumed. Follow the directions supplied with the piece. You are now ready to prime and basepaint your furniture (see page 12).

Sand with 120-grit sandpaper to begin smoothing and cleaning the surface.

Fill depressions and gouges with spackling paste, then sand again.

COLOR AND PATTERN CONSIDERATIONS

Determining which pattern to use involves a combination of your personal preference, the size and shape of the object, and the object's surface characteristics. First, the scale of the pattern should be compatible with the size of the area to be decorated. This is especially true for the edges of surfaces, where some patterns will not work because the surface area is so small. Directional patterns, such as those created with a feather, will only work on very smooth surfaces, whereas a stippled-brush texture will work on surfaces with carving or applied decoration. It is important to consider these relationships and plan ahead accordingly.

I try to follow the guidelines listed at right when choosing color and pattern combinations. You may develop your own choices and combinations. Many of the suggestions in this section are illustrated in the step-by-step examples in part three.

1 Structural elements look best when given the richest or darkest color on a piece.

2 Functional, non-structural elements such as drawers can be lighter and more colorful.

3 Purely decorative elements can be handled as punctuation, with very bold color, or they may be subdued and integrated into the rest of the piece if they are deemed too distracting.

4 Borders around larger areas, such as tabletops and drawer fronts, will lend definition and usually function best if they are darker than the area they border.

5 Areas that have a strong directional pattern should be bordered by more subtle or non-directional textures, and vice versa.

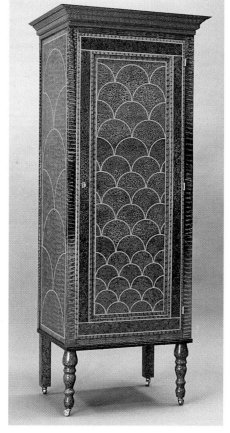

This armoire shows the advantages of flat surfaces and raised panels. The direction of the texture on the raised door frame sets off the motif and pattern of the panels.

The putty texture of the drawers on this small chest follows the horizontal direction of the drawers and suggests the grain pattern of exotic veneer. Darker color on the structural parts offsets the lighter drawers and top.

As for the actual color combinations available, you are limited only by the following:

1 For the technique to be most effective, the base color must be light enough or must have such strong color that it will not be overpowered by the vinegar paint. Very dark or dull base colors will result in muddy or extremely subdued results.

2 Certain pigments have characteristics that make them less desirable to work with. Thalo Blue and Thalo Green, for instance, act like stains and may actually change the base color, thus diminishing the contrast that makes the technique so interesting. For best results, begin with the pigments listed in part one.

3 While tastes in color vary from individual to individual, the traditional ochre base color and earth tone vinegar paints are almost always compatible with any type of furniture.

LINEAR DETAIL AND THE CREATION OF MOTIFS

When you use linear elements in combination with vinegar painted textures, your work will be enriched in the following ways: Lines will form obvious borders around different areas, making transitions and shapes clear. Lines will add emphasis to the elements of a piece of furniture. Lines, since they are a solid color, will provide relief to the eye and add a distinct design quality to the work.

There are two ways in which you can make controlled lines:

• Apply thin masking tape after basecoating, but before vinegar painting. After the vinegar paint has been applied and varnished, remove the tape to reveal a line of the base color. This process allows you a great deal of control, and since the tape will stretch, you can mask curves and irregular shapes.

• Add lines to the varnished surface with specifically designed tools, such as a striping tool or ruling pen. This process allows you to use any color line you wish to complement the base color and vinegar paint. The lining tools may take a little practice to master, but they will work for both straight and curved lines.

Motifs

Motifs may be created for a variety of reasons. A circular motif can lend a focal point. Elliptical motifs can lend elegance to rectangular doors and drawers. Motifs need not be geometric—you can create free-form motifs by drawing directly on the surface with masking tape. By using different colors or textures for the motif and the background, you can mimic the art of inlaid veneering. You can even create representational motifs by using the vinegar paint in a paint-by-number approach.

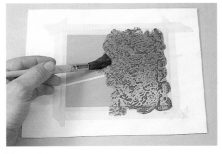

Tape Lines

1 Over the dried basecoat, make a taped or masked line by vinegar painting and varnishing over ⅛″ (.3cm) automotive masking tape.

2 Peel up the tape when the varnish is dry. This process will reveal a line of the base color.

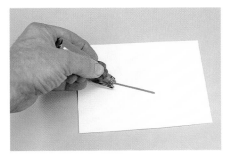

Striping Tool

To create lines in a variety of colors, use a striping tool, which is available from art and craft stores. Slightly thinned latex paint works well with this tool, but you should practice on scrap or sample boards before trying it on your furniture.

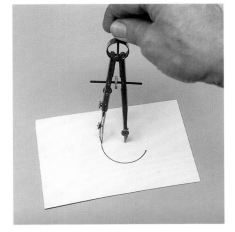

Ruling Pen

Use a ruling pen to create very fine lines and circles with thinned paint. This can be a frustrating tool because of the leaking that sometimes occurs, but when used successfully, it can produce striking effects.

Use both geometric and freeform motifs to highlight structural elements or add design detail. Motifs can be used to emphasize or contrast with the character of the furniture.

PART THREE

Vinegar Painting Step By Step

In this section we will work through a series of projects that will demonstrate the principles and techniques of vinegar painting. These projects show you the procedures you will use to complete your own projects. Of course, your furniture will not look exactly like the pieces I've demonstrated, so you may have to deviate or improvise to accommodate the differences in structure or style.

China Cupboard, 66" tall × 48" wide × 14" deep (1.7m × 1.2m × 35.6cm), collection of the artist

1
SMALL TIN

It's easy to collect a few of these tins from thrift stores, or even from your own closet. They make nice gifts or display containers. You might have to experiment with the paint to get the correct consistency—you don't want it to run off the curved surface. If you have trouble, tape off smaller sections and work on them one at a time so you can control the paint.

YOU WILL NEED:

- Lidded tin
- Primer (close to basecoat color)
- Dark ochre base paint
- Red Oxide vinegar paint
- 220-grit sandpaper
- Fine abrasive pad
- Tack cloth
- No. 2 oval sash brush
- Rubber suction cups
- Varnish and other finishing materials (see part four)

This small, printed tin with a lid is a simple project. It is especially appropriate for beginners or youngsters. Experiment with color and texture to create a variety of results.

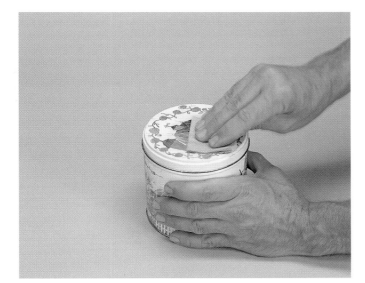

1 To provide a suitable surface for the primer, sand the tin with 220-grit sandpaper and wipe clean with a tack cloth.

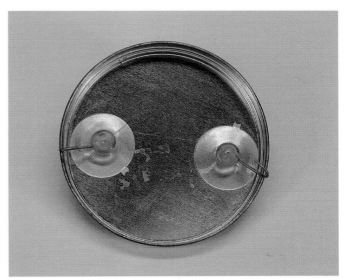

2 Attach one or more small suction cups to the back of the lid for a handhold.

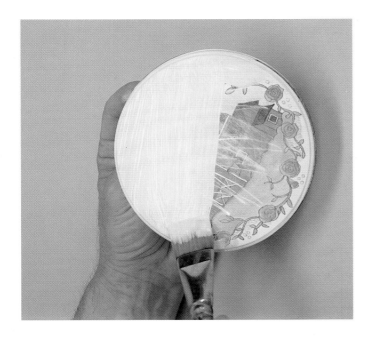

3 Prime the tin using a tinted primer similar to the base color you plan to apply.

4 Give the tin a coat of dark ochre base color.

5 When the first coat is dry, apply a second coat of the base color.

6 Rub the tin with a fine abrasive pad to remove any dust or unevenness in the base color.

7 Insert your hand into the tin to steady it, and apply Red Oxide vinegar paint.

8 After covering the entire tin with the paint, whip a no. 2 oval sash brush vigorously through the paint to create a frothy swirling pattern. If the paint won't froth up, add a tiny amount of soap. Be careful—if you add too much soap, you'll just get colored suds!

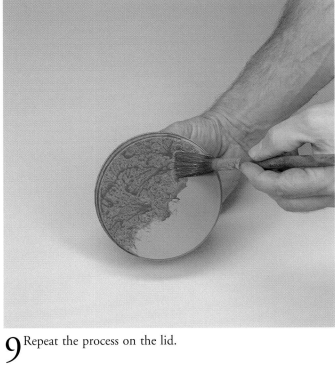

9 Repeat the process on the lid.

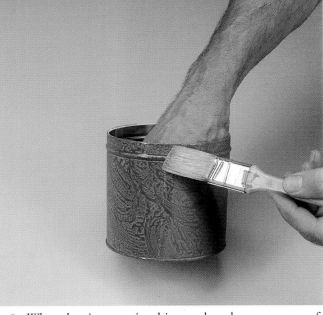

10 When the vinegar paint dries, apply at least two coats of varnish.

2

SHOE BOX

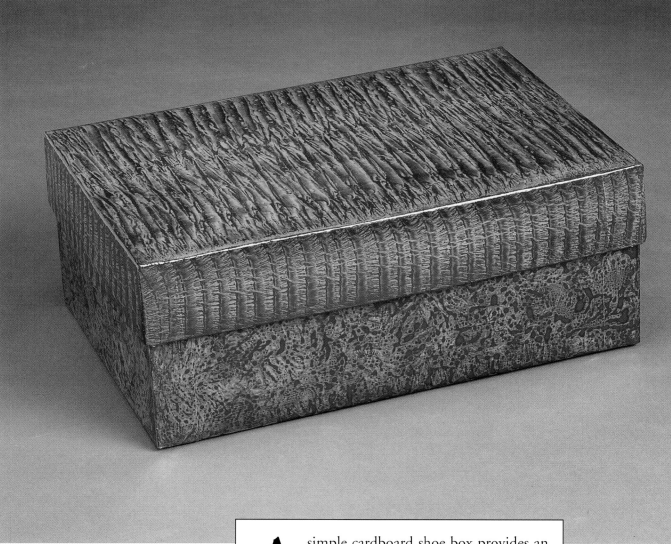

A simple cardboard shoe box provides an inexpensive project on which to practice your vinegar painting techniques. Before you begin, make sure the box and lid fit snugly and there are no loose seams or other damage. Prepare several boxes at the same time to try variations in texture and color, creating a collection to show off or to use for holiday gifts.

A simple, lidded cardboard shoe box, as brought home from the store.

YOU WILL NEED:

• Lidded cardboard shoe box
• Oil-based primer in color similar to base color
• Muralo Pigskin base paint (or other yellow ochre color)
• Burnt Umber vinegar paint
• 150- and 220-grit sandpaper
• Tack cloth
• No. 2 oval sash brush
• Plastic wrap
• Natural-bristle fan brush
• Polyurethane varnish and other finishing materials (see part four)

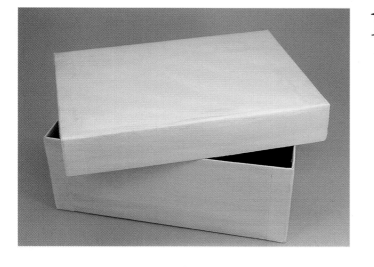

1 Apply a coat of oil-based primer. Water-based latex primer might warp the cardboard or cause the glue to loosen.

2 Sand the box with 150-grit sandpaper to remove brush marks.

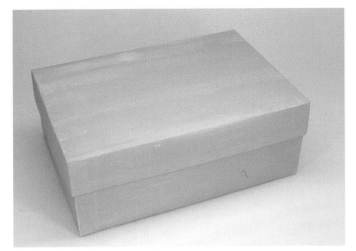

3 Apply one coat of the latex base color. I used Muralo Pigskin. Other colors will give different color effects; for a woody look, choose a base color in the ochre range.

4 Sand the surface with 220-grit sandpaper. Wipe the box with a tack cloth to remove dust. Apply a second coat of the base color.

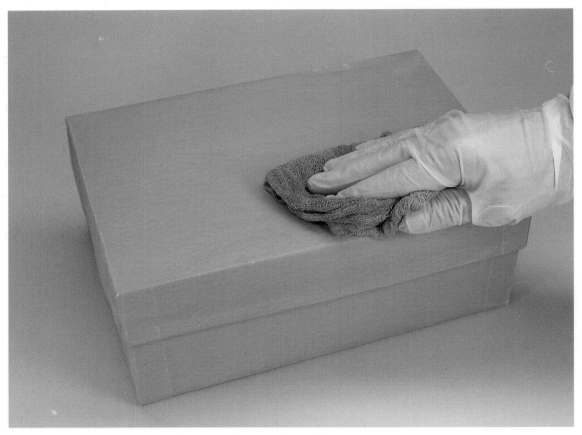

5 Sand again with 220-grit sandpaper and wipe with a tack cloth.

6 Using a no. 2 oval sash brush, apply Burnt Umber vinegar paint to the top surface of the lid, covering half the lid.

7 Move the plastic wrap through the painted section. Leave an area along the center edge untextured.

8 Immediately apply vinegar paint to the other half of the lid, merging the new vinegar paint with the untextured area.

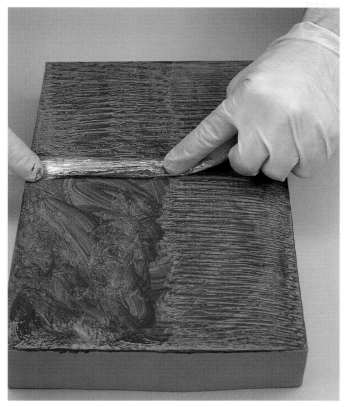

9 Repeat the process with the plastic wrap on the newly painted section of the lid.

10 Allow to dry. Turn the lid on its edge, and apply vinegar paint to the top edge. Texture the edge with a fan brush. Be careful that the vinegar paint doesn't run onto the top of the lid, since this will disturb the dried pattern.

11 After each edge dries, continue the paint-and-texture process until all four edges are completed.

12 Lay the box on its side and apply vinegar paint to the entire surface.

13 Stipple the side vigorously with the no. 2 oval sash brush. Work quickly to complete the entire side before the vinegar paint dries.

14 Allow to dry. Next, turn the box on its end and repeat the application and stippling process. Make sure to let each surface dry thoroughly before moving on. Cover the entire box.

15 Apply polyurethane varnish to the top surface of the lid. Varnish the edges of the lid and the sides of the box. Allow to dry.

3

PICTURE FRAME WITH RAISED CORNERS

This small picture frame has separate block corners, giving you the opportunity to develop a different color and texture to set off the rest of the finish. Be on the lookout for items to paint that, while essentially flat, have some surface variation you can highlight in this way.

YOU WILL NEED:

- Picture frame with raised corners
- Primer in a color similar to base paint
- Burnt orange base paint
- Manganese Violet vinegar paint
- Alizarin Crimson vinegar paint
- 150- and 220-grit sandpaper
- Fine abrasive pad
- #0000 steel wool
- Tack cloth
- No. 2 oval sash brush
- ¾" (1.9cm) drafting tape
- Glazing compound
- Varnish and other finishing materials (see part four)

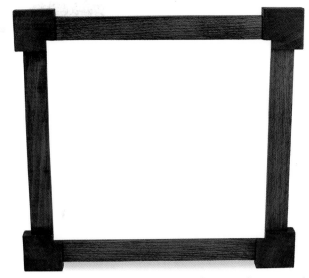

This frame is a good choice to decorate because the corner detail provides a natural place to vary the textures and colors.

1 Sand the frame with medium (150-grit) sandpaper.

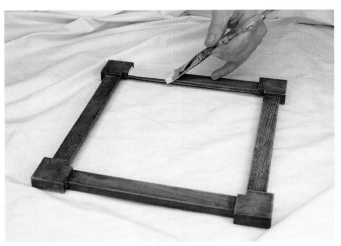

2 Prime the frame in a color similar to the base paint.

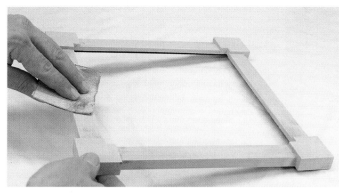

3 When dry, sand again with 150-grit sandpaper.

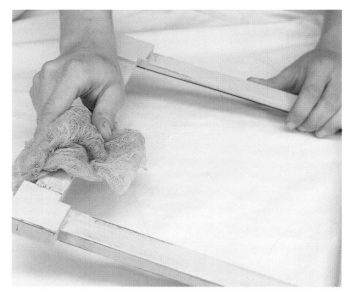

4 Wipe the frame with a tack cloth to remove dust.

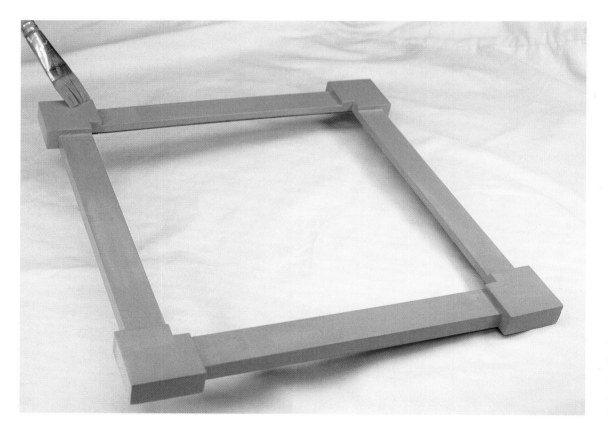

5 Apply two coats of Burnt Orange base color. When dry, rub with a fine-grade abrasive pad or 220-grit sandpaper.

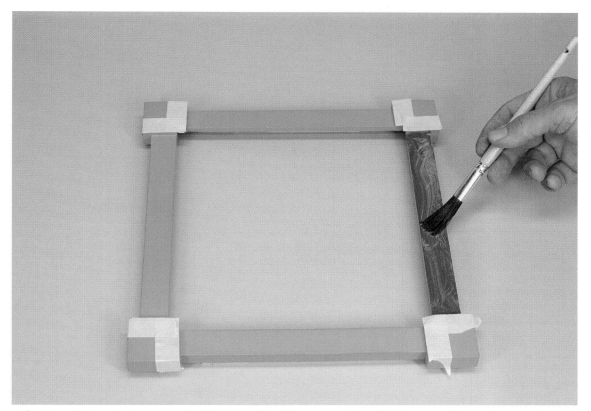

6 Mask off the raised corners with ¾" (1.9cm) drafting tape and apply Manganese Violet vinegar paint to one of the unmasked areas, including the frame edge.

7 Immediately texture these surfaces with the no. 2 oval sash brush by tapping the side of the brush into the paint as you move along.

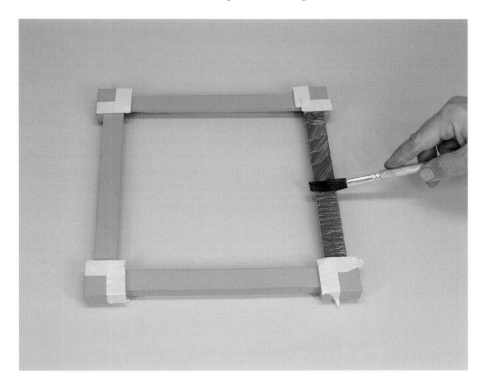

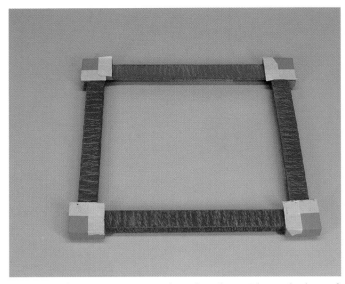

8 Apply the same texture to the other three sides and edges of the frame.

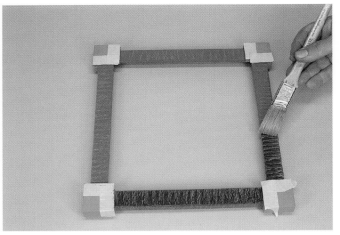

9 Varnish all four sides and edges after the vinegar paint dries.

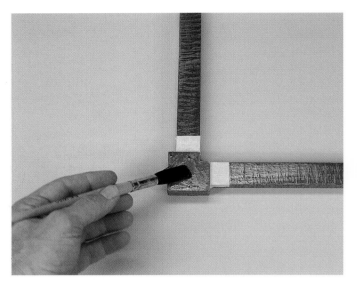

10 Remove the ¾″ (1.9cm) drafting tape from the corners and apply more tape to the varnished areas. Brush Alizarin Crimson vinegar paint onto one corner.

11 Immediately texture the wet paint by tapping a small piece of glazing compound through the paint in a diagonal direction. Do the edges at this time, also. They can be stippled with the same brush used to apply the vinegar paint.

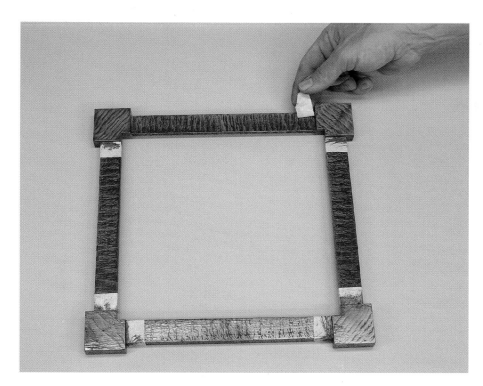

12 Repeat this process on all four corners and varnish when dry. Carefully take off the drafting tape from the sides and apply a second coat of varnish to the entire frame, including the sides, edges and corners.

13 After the varnish dries, rub the frame with #0000 steel wool, being careful not to rub through the finish. Use a small piece of steel wool to rub the edges of the frame.

14 Apply a third coat of varnish to finish this project.

4

PICTURE FRAME WITH LINER

Frames like this can be found at home centers and department stores, costing a fraction of what you would pay for more elaborately decorated frames. If the frame is painted, try using the color as a base color. Choose your own base color if the frame is unfinished. Avoid fancy carving or detail.

YOU WILL NEED:

- 5″ × 7″ (12.7cm × 17.8cm) picture frame with detachable liner
- Burnt Sienna vinegar paint
- #0000 steel wool
- Tack cloth
- No. 2 oval sash brush
- ¾″ (1.9cm) drafting tape
- Glazing compound
- Varnish and other finishing materials (see part four)

1 Disassemble the frame and rub the surface of the large yellow part with #0000 grade steel wool. Wipe clean with a tack cloth. The existing yellow will provide the basecoat for the vinegar paint. I decided to leave the liner bright red.

This 5″ × 7″ (12.7cm × 17.8cm) picture frame with a detachable liner was already finished in these bright colors.

2 Use ¾″ (1.9cm) drafting tape at the corners to mask off two sides of the frame.

3 Brush Burnt Sienna vinegar paint onto one of the masked-off sides.

4 Then, using a small piece of glazing compound, stamp a series of overlapping linear marks into the vinegar paint.

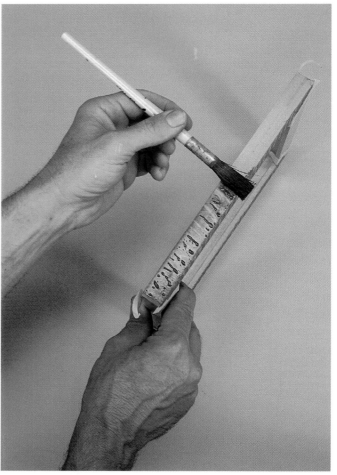

5 Use the side of the no. 2 sash brush to simultaneously apply and texture the vinegar paint on the edge of the frame.

6 Repeat this process on the opposite side of the frame.

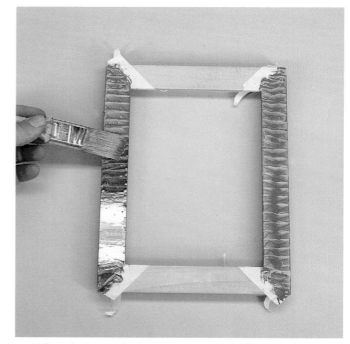

7 When dry, varnish the vinegar painted sides and edges.

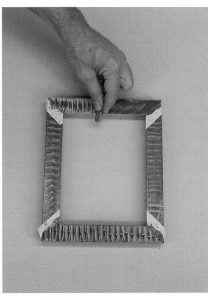

8 After the varnish dries, move the tape to the varnished sides of the frame.

9 Repeat the painting process on the two remaining sides and edges of the frame.

10 Varnish these areas when dry.

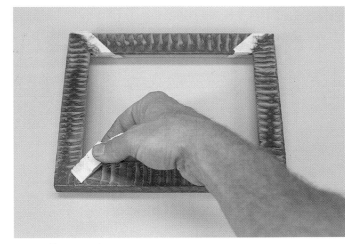

11 Remove the tape.

12 Lightly rub the surface with #0000 steel wool and wipe with the tack cloth.

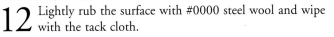

13 Apply one or more coats of varnish to complete the finish. Reassemble the frame with the liner to complete the project.

5

LAZY SUSAN

This lazy Susan is made of molded composition material and originally had a printed woodgrain finish. Damage to the original finish makes this type of object an ideal candidate for vinegar painting. Other small accessories for the kitchen, dining room or home office would also work well.

YOU WILL NEED:

- Lazy Susan
- Ochre-tinted primer
- Yellow ochre (Pigskin) latex enamel
- Burnt Sienna vinegar paint
- Burnt Umber vinegar paint
- Prussian Blue vinegar paint
- 150- and 220-grit sandpaper
- #0000 steel wool
- Tack cloth

- No. 2 oval sash brush
- ⅛″ (.3cm) automotive masking tape
- ¼″ (.6cm) drafting tape
- Drafting compass
- Razor blade or craft knife
- No. 4 watercolor brush
- No. 4 natural-bristle fan brush
- Varnish and other finishing materials

This lazy Susan, a flea market purchase with some slight surface damage, provides a good starting point for a vinegar painting project.

1 Sand the surface damage smooth with 150-grit sandpaper and wipe clean with a tack cloth.

2 Prime the lazy Susan with ochre-tinted latex primer and sand smooth with 150-grit sandpaper when dry.

3 Basecoat the lazy Susan with yellow ochre latex enamel (Muralo Pigskin) and sand with 220-grit sandpaper to smooth the surface.

4 If the color is uneven, apply a second coat and resand. Wipe clean after each sanding.

5 Use a drafting compass to draw a line about 1½" (3.8cm) in from the edge of the lazy Susan. Keep the pointed leg of the compass positioned against the outside edge of the lazy Susan. While holding the compass vertically, rotate the lazy Susan to create the line.

6 To provide linear detail to the design, apply ⅛" (.3cm) automotive masking tape outside the drawn line. Keep tension on the tape as you press it down to prevent it from wrinkling as you proceed around the circle.

7 Overlap the tape at the end of the circle, and carefully trim it by pulling the tape up against a razor blade. Trimming the tape this way prevents you from accidentally cutting into the painted surface.

8 Seal the tape by brushing over it with a thin coat of the base color. This will prevent vinegar paint from leaking under the tape.

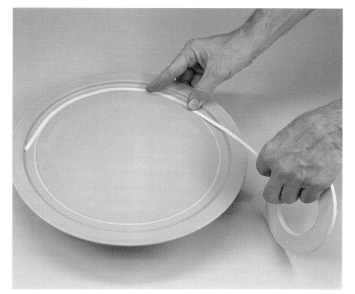

9 Use ¼″ (.6cm) drafting tape to mask around the outside of the ⅛″ (.3cm) tape. Wider tape could be used for this purpose, but it is more difficult to manipulate. This tape will protect the outer rim of the lazy Susan for your second color. Overlap the ⅛″ (.3cm) tape as you begin and continue to apply as many widths of the ¼″ (.6cm) tape as you feel are necessary to prevent yourself from accidentally brushing the vinegar paint onto the border.

10 Apply Burnt Sienna vinegar paint inside the taped border. Stipple the paint with a no. 2 oval sash brush. For a small area like this, you may be able to do both actions at once, stippling the vinegar paint directly onto the inner circle of the lazy Susan. As you complete the entire area, work quickly to maintain a wet edge so the texture will be consistent.

11 After the vinegar paint dries, varnish this area. After the varnish dries, check for holidays (small unvarnished areas) and revarnish, if necessary.

12 When dry, remove the ¼″ (.6cm) tape from the border area. Be careful not to pull up the ⅛″ (.3cm) tape. Apply the ¼″ (.6cm) tape to the varnished area. As before, keep tension on the tape to prevent wrinkling and use as many tape widths as necessary to protect the inner circle.

13 Brush Burnt Umber vinegar paint onto the entire border area of the lazy Susan.

14 While the Burnt Umber vinegar paint is still wet, use a no. 4 watercolor brush to quickly touch in spots of Prussian Blue vinegar paint. These spots of Prussian Blue should be randomly distributed, approximately 1″ to 2″ (2.5cm to 5cm) apart.

15 Use a no. 4 natural-bristle fan brush to texture around the outside of the tape. As you move the brush along, lay it almost flat and tap the side of the brush into the paint, leaving a series of curved marks with the tip. While you are doing this, the two colors will join together to make an interesting combination. Complete one revolution in this fashion.

16 Now reverse the direction of the brush and make a second row of marks around the rim of the lazy Susan in the opposite direction. Reversing the brush direction creates an elegant S-curve pattern in the vinegar paint.

17 Varnish this area after the vinegar paint has dried.

18 When the varnish has dried thoroughly, carefully remove all the tape.

19 As you pull up the ⅛″ (.3cm) tape, the linear detail of basecoat color is revealed.

20 Turn the lazy Susan over. Basecoat as before, let dry and stipple with Burnt Umber vinegar paint.

21 Varnish the underside for a finished appearance.

22 Return to the top of the lazy Susan and apply at least one more coat of varnish. This protects the linear detail and builds a more durable finish.

23 After the final coat of varnish has dried, rub the surface with #0000 steel wool pad to complete the project.

6

SERVING TRAY WITH OVAL MOTIF

You can probably find a small tray similar to this one at a flea market or thrift shop. The small size makes it a good project for a beginner, and the flat area gives you the opportunity to create a design motif, such as the ellipse used here. The completed project can be displayed or put to practical use.

This small serving tray was purchased for a few dollars at a thrift store. The finish showed some damage and water stains.

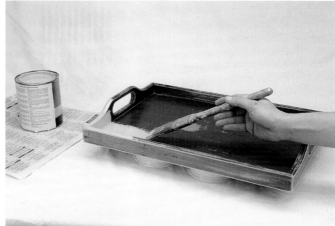

1 Remove the small corner braces by carefully prying out the nails, and then sand the tray with 150-grit sandpaper. Prime the tray with an ochre-tinted primer, which will be more compatible with the base color.

2 Give the tray two coats of bright orange latex enamel. Sand with fine (220-grit) sandpaper after each coat and wipe or brush off all dust.

3 Make an oval template out of light cardboard and center it on the tray. Draw around the template with a graphite pencil, pressing lightly.

YOU WILL NEED:

- Small serving tray
- Ochre-tinted primer
- Bright orange latex enamel
- Alizarin Crimson vinegar paint
- Prussian Blue vinegar paint
- Black vinegar paint
- 150- and 220-grit sandpaper
- Tack cloth

- No. 2 oval sash brush
- ⅛" (.6cm) automotive masking tape
- ¾" (1.9cm) drafting tape
- Light cardboard for template
- Graphite pencil
- 3-inch (7.6cm) foam brush
- Damp cloth
- Varnish and other finishing materials

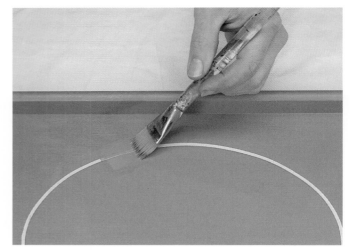

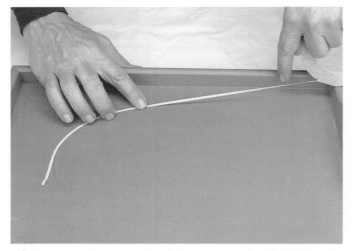

4 Tape around the outside of the drawn oval with ⅛″ (.3cm) automotive masking tape. As you apply the tape, be sure to stretch it slightly to keep it from wrinkling.

5 Press the tape tightly to the surface, and lay on a thin coat of orange paint directly over the tape. This paint will seal the edges of the tape and give a crisp edge to your design.

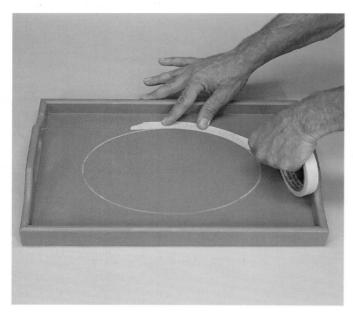

6 After the paint on the ⅛″ (.3cm) tape has dried, use ¾″ (1.9cm) drafting tape to mask around the outside of the oval. Use several short, overlapping pieces to accomplish this. At the same time, mask off the flat part of the tray from the sides.

7 Use the no. 2 oval sash brush to stipple Alizarin Crimson vinegar paint onto the oval area.

9 Restipple the area. This will provide a subtle color variation within the stippled pattern. After the vinegar paint dries, varnish this area. The Alizarin pigment tends to be gritty, so these areas may need to be sanded and revarnished a few times to achieve a smooth finish.

8 While the Alizarin Crimson paint is still wet, touch in small spots of Prussian Blue.

10 Tape off opposite ends of the tray at the corners and stipple these two sides with the Alizarin Crimson. Do the interior and the exterior at the same time. If the vinegar paint dries slowly, use a hair dryer to speed the drying. Be careful not to blow the vinegar paint around or you will disturb the stippled pattern. Varnish the two sides and let dry.

11 Remove the drafting tape from around the oval and from the corners.

12 Now mask off the sides which have already been vinegar painted and varnished.

13 Stipple the ends of the tray with the Alizarin Crimson vinegar paint and varnish them as you did on the other sides.

14 After the varnish dries, carefully remove all the drafting tape and wipe the undecorated area with a damp cloth to remove any splatters.

15 Place drafting tape over the varnished areas adjacent to the undecorated part of the tray.

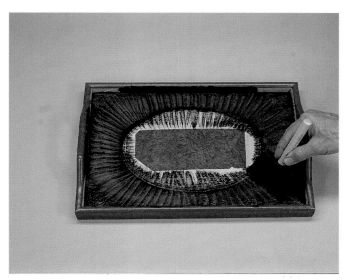

16 Add extra pieces of tape to give the finished areas as much protection as needed. Quickly brush black vinegar paint onto the undecorated area of the tray.

17 While this paint is still wet, use a 3-inch (7.6cm) foam brush that has been dipped into black vinegar paint to create a series of rays around the oval. Experiment with different ways of holding the brush and briskly striking the surface until you achieve the desired linear effect. Take a few strokes of the brush into each corner to complete the effect.

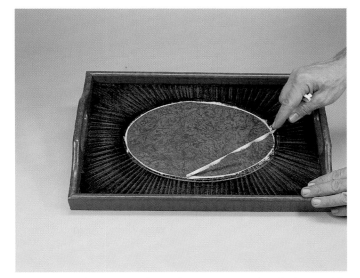

18 Varnish this area after it dries. Be sure to brush the varnish into the corners and along the edges. Two coats provide a good seal. Carefully remove all the drafting tape from the tray.

19 Remove the ⅛″ (.3cm) tape to reveal a line of the base color. Wipe the surface with a damp cloth to remove drips or splashes of vinegar paint, and varnish the entire tray one or more times to provide a durable finish. Reattach the corner braces to finish the tray.

7

SERVING TRAY WITH DIAMOND MOTIF

A big serving tray like this one is great for taking refreshments to a summer porch gathering—choosing a summery, green color combination helps keep things cool. The diamond motif sets off the rectangular shape of the tray. Apply a couple of extra coats of varnish to any item you'll be using frequently.

1 Prime this large, wooden serving tray with gray primer, which is closer to the tone of the base paint. Matching the primer to the base paint will give the tray a more uniform color. Sand with 150-grit sandpaper and wipe with a tack cloth.

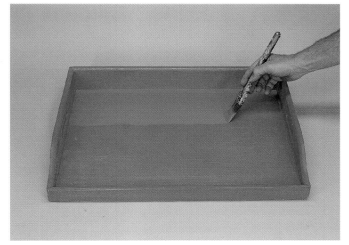

2 Basecoat the tray with Teal Green latex enamel (Benjamin Moore 658). Apply two coats, sanding after each coat.

3 Cut a diamond-shaped template from a piece of light cardboard and position it in the middle of the tray. With a sharp pencil, trace a line around the template.

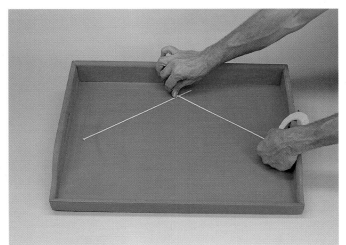

4 Apply ⅛" (.3cm) automotive masking tape around the pencil lines.

5 Trim the corners by pulling the tape up against a razor blade.

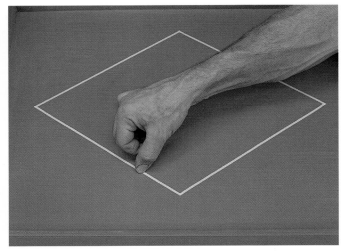

6 Burnish the tape thoroughly.

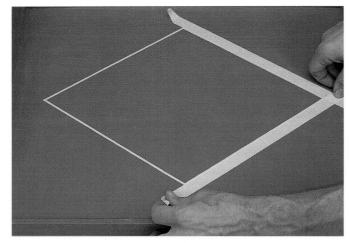

7 Use ¾″ (1.9cm) drafting tape to reinforce the thin masking tape.

8 Mask off the edges of the tray.

9 Use a craft stick to push the drafting tape into the corners.

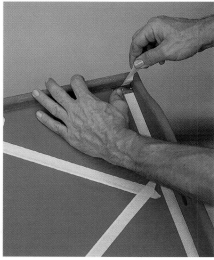

10 Trim the tape by pulling it up against a razor blade.

YOU WILL NEED:

- Large serving tray
- Gray primer
- Teal Green latex enamel (Benjamin Moore 658)
- 4 parts Viridian Green to 1 part Mars Black vinegar paint
- 1 part Cobalt Blue to 1 part Titanium White vinegar paint
- 150- and 220-grit sandpaper
- #0000 steel wool or fine abrasive pad
- Tack cloth
- No. 2 oval sash brush
- ⅛″ (.3cm) automotive masking tape
- ¾″ (1.9cm) drafting tape
- 1½″ (3.8cm) painter's tape
- Craft stick
- Razor blade or craft knife
- Newspaper
- Light cardboard for template
- Graphite pencil
- 3-inch (7.6cm) foam brush
- Turkey quill
- Cotton swab and vinegar, if needed
- Varnish and other finishing materials (see part four)

11 Place 1½″ (3.8cm) wide painter's tape around the diamond motif to keep the vinegar paint off this area.

12 Make a mix of vinegar paint using four parts Viridian Green to one part Mars Black. Brush the mixture loosely into the diamond area.

13 Dampen a turkey quill with this mixture, and press it into the vinegar paint to create a linear pattern. Work from one direction and then the other to balance the pattern.

14 When dry, seal the area with a coat of varnish.

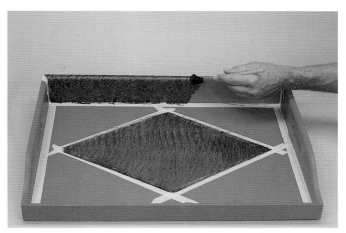

15 Use ¾" (1.9cm) drafting tape to protect the ends of the tray. Stipple inside the front and on the back of the tray with the green-black mixture. Varnish when dry.

16 After the varnish dries, move the tape onto the finished sides and stipple the remaining ends. Varnish when dry. You may be tempted to paint the inside of the tray all at once, but inside corners are difficult to do in one pass as you can easily smear the finished side as you work on the next side.

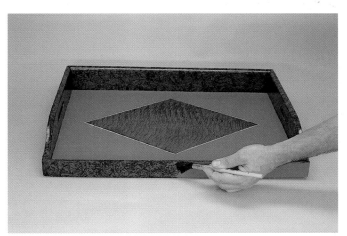

17 Now stipple the outside of all four sides. It isn't necessary to tape off the outside corners because you are less likely to disturb the texture as you move from one side to the next.

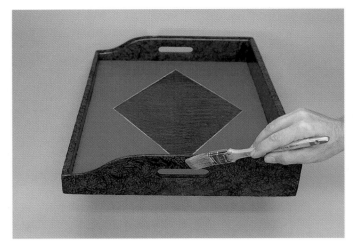

18 Varnish the outside.

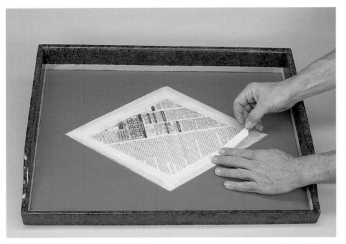

19 Before painting around the motif, protect the sides of the tray with ¾" (1.9cm) drafting tape. Also cover the motif with drafting tape and newspaper so you can work freely around it.

20 Create a vinegar paint mixture of one part Cobalt Blue to one part Titanium White. Brush this partway around the diamond motif.

21 Dampen a 3-inch (7.6cm) foam brush with some of the light blue mixture, and press it into the wet surface to create a linear pattern from end to end.

22 Add more light blue vinegar paint as you move to the next part of the surface and continue patterning until the entire area is complete.

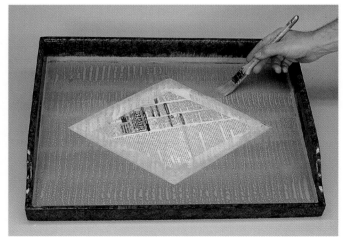

23 When the paint is dry, varnish the entire area.

24 Carefully remove all of the tape and newspaper from the tray.

25 A line of the base color is revealed as the ⅛″ (.3cm) tape is removed.

26 Use a cotton swab dipped in vinegar to clean up paint that might have leaked under the thin tape.

27 Rub down the entire piece with a #0000 steel wool pad.

28 Give the tray one or more coats of varnish to complete the project.

8

MAPLE BOX

This interesting box was probably intended to hold art supplies. Check secondhand stores for a similar box or art supply stores for a new box. Maple is a good wood to paint because it is fine-grained and hard, but almost any kind of wood is fine for a small item like this. The challenge and fun of this project is to make the simple box look as though it is inlaid with different types of veneer. When designing your finish, be sure to consider the way the top and bottom of the box will look together.

A simple maple box found at a flea market.

1 Remove the hinges and hardware from the box. Sand the box with 150-grit sandpaper to clean and smooth the surface. Wipe the box with a cloth dipped in naphtha or mineral spirits to remove wax or other residue.

2 Prime the box with an ochre-tinted primer and sand with 220-grit sandpaper when dry. Basecoat the box with yellow ochre latex enamel (different manufacturers will have different names for this color; both Muralo and Pittsburgh Paints call this color Pigskin) and sand when dry.

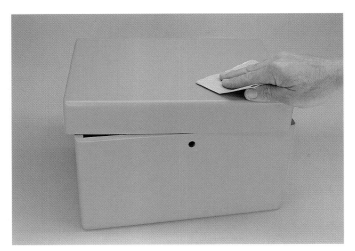

3 Repeat the basecoating and sanding process.

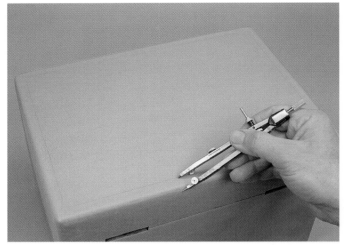

4 Using a compass, draw lines about ¾″ (1.9cm) from the edge of the box to mark off the borders.

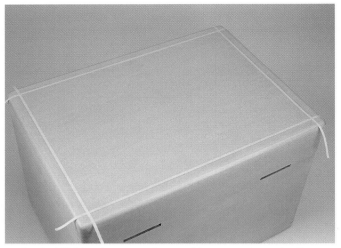

5 Apply ⅛″ (.3cm) automotive masking tape along the lines. Create a rectangular border around the top, and trim the corners by lifting the tape up against a razor blade.

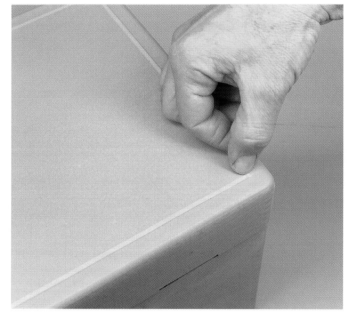

6 Burnish the tape with your fingernail or a craft stick. Pay particular attention to the corners, where the masking tape overlaps. Burnishing prevents the vinegar paint from running underneath the tape.

7 On the outside of the border but overlapping the thin tape, apply ¾″ (1.9cm) drafting tape to protect this area. This will allow you to work freely without worrying about going over the line of ⅛″ tape.

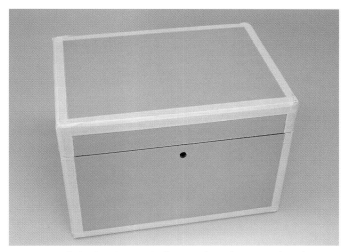

8 Draw and tape similar borders on the front, back and ends. Hold the lid closed with rubber bands or plastic wrap to make sure the lines match up.

9 Tape off the borders as before so that the entire box has borders covered with the ¾″ tape.

10 Brush Burnt Sienna vinegar paint onto the lid.

11 Texture with a large, natural-bristle fan brush. Reverse directions with each row of brush marks so that a serpentine line is created. When the lid is dry, apply two coats of varnish.

12 Apply Burnt Sienna vinegar paint to the end of the box.

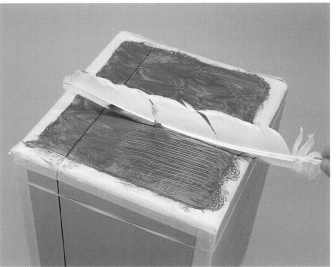

13 Use a trimmed turkey feather to stipple this surface.

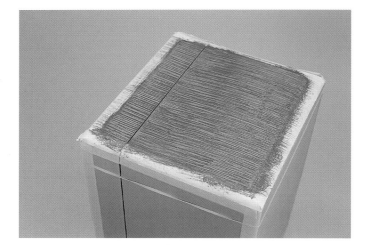

14 Reverse the direction of the feather for the second row of stipples so that a curved or serpentine line is created, similar in character to the line on the lid. Varnish when dry. Be careful not to put so much varnish on that it runs in the crack between the bottom and the lid. If this seems difficult, remove the rubber bands and varnish the parts separately. Texture the other end and back of the box in a similar manner, changing position of the rubber bands as needed.

15 Cover the front of the box with Burnt Sienna.

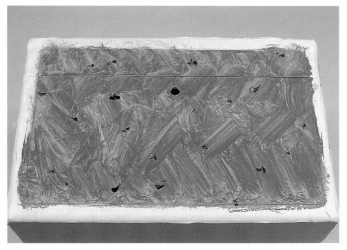

16 Just before texturing with the feather, touch in small dots of Prussian Blue.

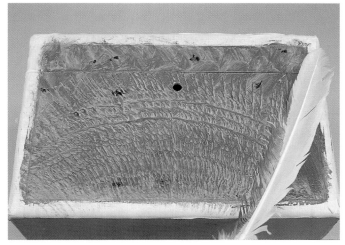

17 Using an untrimmed feather, stipple the front in a fan pattern.

18 You may need to make two or three passes. Notice that the Prussian Blue has been worked into the Burnt Sienna to create a subtle organic effect. Apply two coats of varnish to the front.

19 Remove the top of the box and turn it over. Paint and varnish the edges where the top and bottom of the box meet.

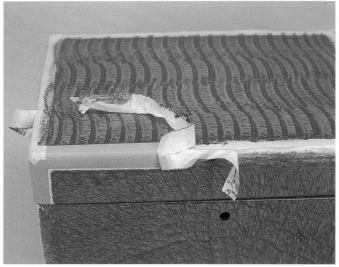

20 After the varnished edges have dried, remove the wide drafting tape from the borders.

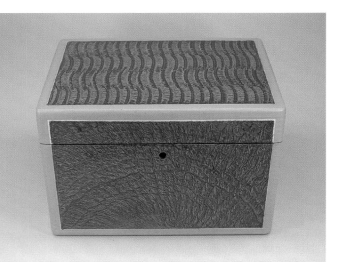

21 Be careful not to pull up the thin masking tape lines.

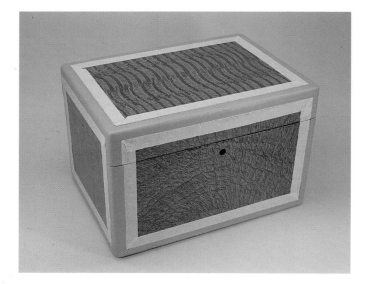

22 Apply drafting tape to the other side of the thin masking tape to protect the finished areas. You are now ready to paint the borders.

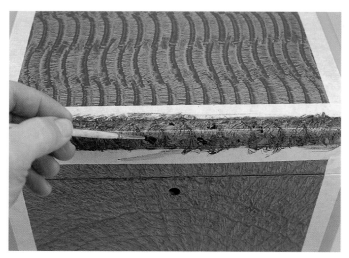

23 Brush Burnt Umber vinegar paint on the border. Touch in small dots of Prussian Blue.

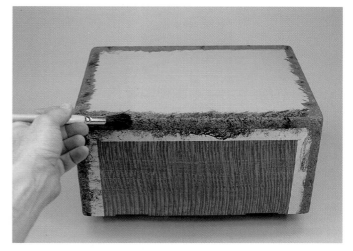

24 Stipple the area with a no. 2 oval sash brush to blend the dots of Prussian Blue into the Burnt Umber. Varnish the lid and set it aside

25 Turn the box upside down and texture the borders of the bottom using the same process used on the lid. Make sure to catch part of the underside. Varnish the completed borders. When the box is dry, turn it right side up.

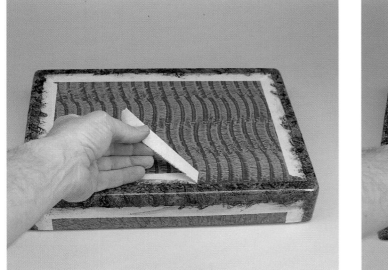

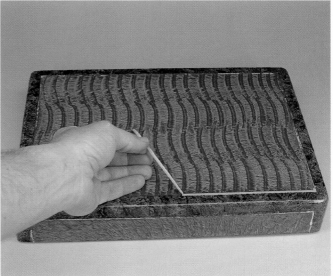

26 Carefully remove the wide drafting and narrow masking tapes. Apply two more coats of varnish to the box and reassemble.

9

SILVERWARE BOX

Although they are designed to hold silver-ware, these boxes also make good jew-elry boxes. This project demonstrates a more complex, two-layer process which approxi-mates the look of crotched mahogany. The bor-ders have some of the visual qualities of satin-wood. Practice these techniques on a sample board before starting on the box. The brushes required to create these effects are more expensive than the other vinegar painting tools, but they will allow for more sophisticated effects.

1 Sand, prime and basecoat an old silverware box that has a drawer (refer to instructions on the previous project).

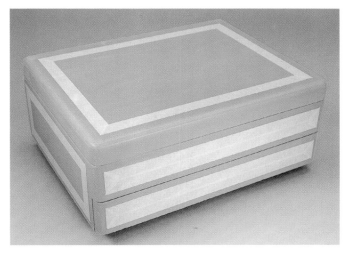

2 As in the previous project, create borders around the top ends and front panels with ⅛" (.3cm) masking tape. Protect the areas inside the borders with ¾" (1.9cm) drafting tape.

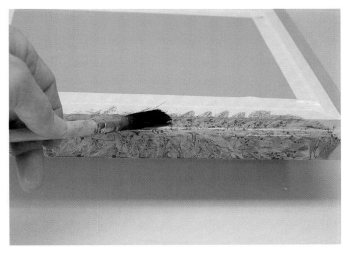

3 Use the no. 2 oval sash brush on its side to stipple the borders with Kremer Transparent Red #5240. This will create a coppery effect similar to satinwood over the base color.

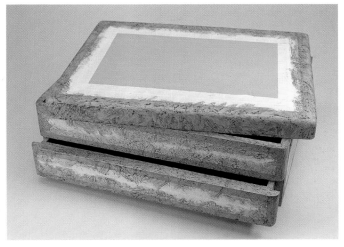

4 When dry, apply two coats of varnish to all borders.

YOU WILL NEED:

- Silverware box with drawer
- Ochre-tinted primer
- Yellow ochre (Pigskin) base paint
- Kremer Transparent Red #5240 vinegar paint
- 1 part Transparent Red to 1 part Mars Black vinegar paint
- 2 parts Alizarin Crimson to 1 part Mars Black vinegar paint
- 150- and 220-grit sandpaper
- Abrasive pad
- Cloth and naphtha or mineral spirits
- ⅛" (.3cm) automotive masking tape
- ¾" (1.9cm) drafting tape
- No. 2 oval sash brush
- Glazing compound or putty
- Plastic wrap
- Flogging brush
- Badger blender brush
- Turkey quill
- Varnish and other finishing materials (see part four)

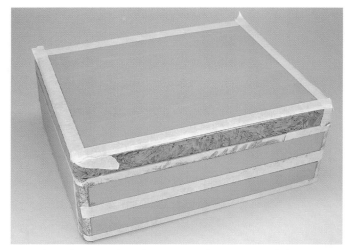

5 When the varnish is dry, reverse the position of the wide drafting tape to protect the finished borders.

6 Paint the top with a vinegar paint mixture of one part Transparent Red to one part Mars Black.

7 Use a finger-shaped piece of glazing compound or putty to stamp a series of arcs across the top.

8 Apply two coats of varnish to this area. After the varnish dries, rub with an abrasive pad to dull the glossy surface. This is important—otherwise the vinegar paint will bead up and will not hold a pattern.

9 Apply a second layer of vinegar paint to the top, comprised of two parts Alizarin Crimson to one part Mars Black.

10 Use the no. 2 oval sash brush to establish a series of curved lines, following the general pattern of the arcs in the first layer of paint. Work quickly to complete the following steps before the vinegar paint dries.

11 With the side of the brush, lay in additional vinegar paint near the center of the arcs.

12 Dab these areas with a crumpled piece of plastic wrap to suggest the rays of crotched mahogany.

13 Texture the entire area by lightly patting it with a flogging brush.

14 Brush over the area with a badger blender to soften the edges.

15 The dried pattern may look very dense, but it should exhibit the complex arched pattern. Varnish the area to bring out the underlying pattern and color to complete the effect.

16 Remove the ¾" (1.9cm) drafting tape to reveal the dramatic variation of color and texture between the center and border.

17 Remove the ⅛" (.3cm) masking tape and varnish.

18 Paint the end panels, one at a time, with the mixture of one part Transparent Red to one part Mars Black.

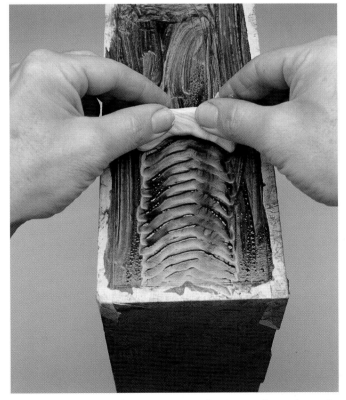

19 Use putty or glazing compound to cover the end panels with a series of arcs.

20 When the paint has dried, apply two coats of varnish and rub with the abrasive pad.

21 For a slightly different and quicker effect, apply the second layer of vinegar paint (two parts Alizarin Crimson to one part Mars Black) and comb through it with a turkey quill to simulate a straight-grained pattern.

22 Soften with the badger blender. When dry, apply two coats of varnish.

23 Remove the wide drafting and narrow masking tapes and varnish again.

24 Complete the front panels in a similar fashion.

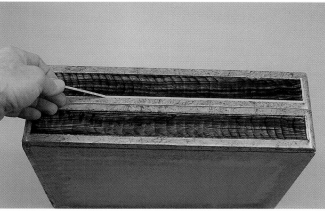

25 Remove the tape from this area.

26 Be sure to rub all the parts with an abrasive pad before applying additional coats of varnish. Replace the hardware to finish the project.

10

SMALL COCKTAIL TABLE WITH SHELF

A small table like this provides a great opportunity to have some fun with a more involved design. The large, flat top gives you plenty of space to try out some different shapes and patterns. By adding lines with the ruling pen and lining tools, you can create exciting color effects.

1 Prime the table with gray primer, and sand with 220-grit sandpaper.

2 Basecoat this table in Pratt and Lambert #1205 or a similar blue paint. Sand with 150-grit sandpaper, wipe with a tack cloth and recoat, if necessary. Remove the shelf and paint it separately (see step 21).

This sample board shows several options for color and texture.

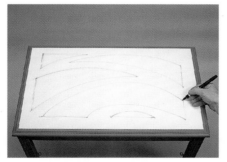

3 Create a design motif for the top of the table by sketching on a piece of railroad board. Keep the shapes simple so the masking will not be too complex.

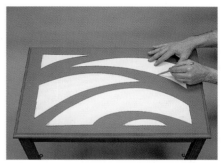

4 Cut the shapes out of the railroad board and lay them on the table in a pleasing arrangement. Trace around them with a pencil to transfer the design to the tabletop.

YOU WILL NEED:

- Small cocktail table with shelf
- Gray primer
- Pratt and Lambert #1205 or similar blue base paint
- Manganese Violet vinegar paint
- Alizarin Crimson vinegar paint
- Turquoise latex paint
- 150- and 220-grit sandpaper
- Tack cloth
- ⅛″ (.3cm) automotive masking tape
- ¾″ (1.9cm) drafting tape

- Craft knife
- No. 2 oval sash brush
- Railroad board
- Pencil
- Plastic wrap
- Liner tool
- Ruling pen
- Compass
- 2-inch (5.1cm) foam brush
- Varnish and other finishing materials (see part four)

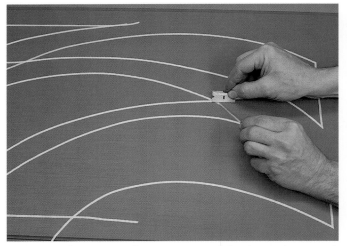

5 Apply ⅛″ (.3cm) masking tape around the drawn design and trim the tape by lifting the ends against a razor blade.

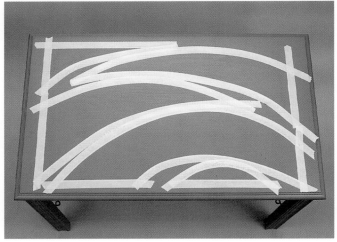

6 Mask the exterior of the shapes using ¾″ (1.9cm) drafting tape.

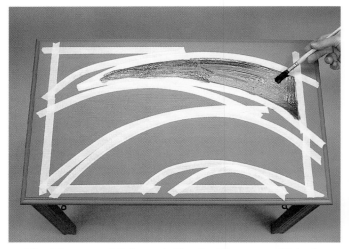

7 Use Manganese Violet and Alizarin Crimson to fill in the positive areas of the design, blending the colors in some areas and using them individually in other areas.

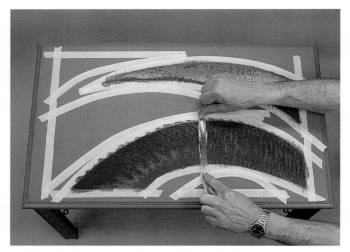

8 Use plastic wrap and the stippling technique to create a variety of textures.

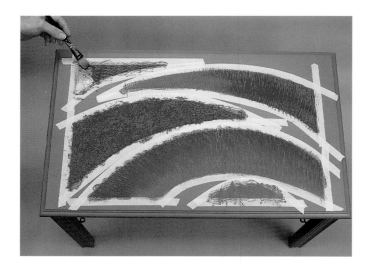

9 Wipe up any paint that has escaped the borders and varnish the positive areas of the design.

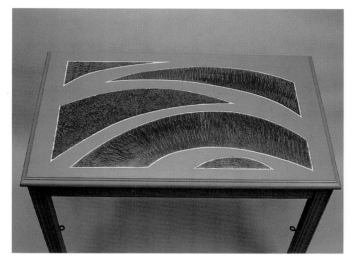

10 Remove the wide drafting tape from outside the borders.

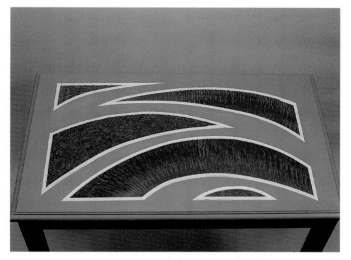

11 Place the drafting tape on the inside of the ⅛″ (.3cm) tape.

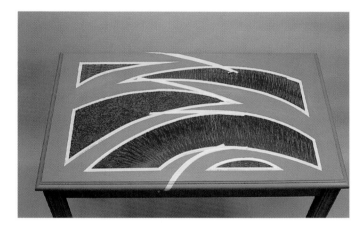

12 Because the background is a somewhat elaborate shape, subdivide it using the ¾″ (1.9cm) drafting tape. This will allow you to work carefully without having to cover the entire surface while the paint is wet.

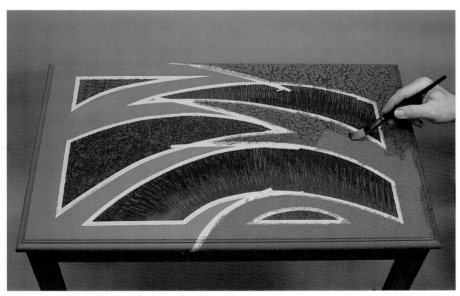

13 Stipple one area of the background with the Manganese Violet, and apply one coat of varnish.

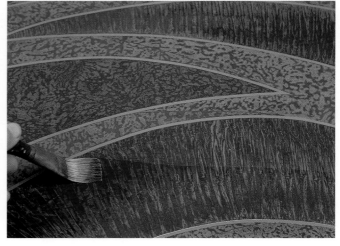

14 When the varnish is dry, move the tape onto the stippled and varnished area. Stipple in the rest of the background with the Manganese Violet, and apply one coat of varnish.

15 Remove all of the tape and give the whole surface a coat of varnish. Notice that although the two background sections of the tabletop have a minor textural variation, they still blend together very effectively.

16 To create a linear border with a different color, use the liner tool and turquoise latex paint. Practice with the liner tool on scrap paper until you are able to achieve a consistent, fluid line. Then, placing the guide against the edge of the table, draw the border one side at a time until you have worked your way around the tabletop.

17 Use a ruling pen to create another type of linear detail. The same turquoise latex paint that was used for the border can be thinned down and brushed into the ruling pen. Practice thinning the paint and applying it into the ruling pen with a small brush until you are able to achieve a consistent result. With the ruling pen attached to a compass, small circles can be added to the design for emphasis.

18 Here is the completed tabletop, showing the blended design shapes, the linear border and the circular detailing. Apply a final coat of varnish.

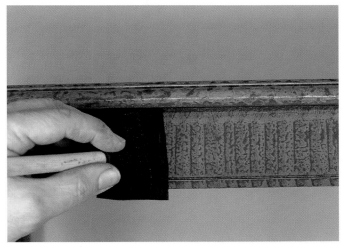

19 Paint the apron of the table using Alizarin Crimson vinegar paint and a 2-inch (5.1cm) foam brush to create a linear pattern. Varnish when dry.

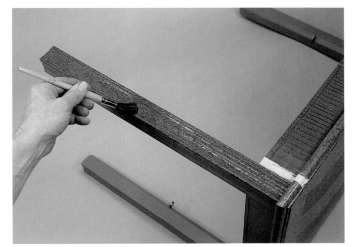

20 Using the same color, stipple the top surface of the legs and apply a coat of varnish. Continue working on the table apron and the legs by turning the table a quarter turn and painting the horizontal surfaces until all four sides are completed.

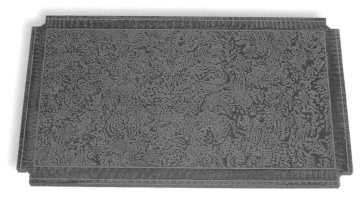

21 Use the same colors and turquoise border to complete the shelf. Reinstall the shelf to complete the project.

11

TWO-DRAWER NIGHTSTAND

Y ou will find many small stands, originally
part of a bedroom set, available as inexpensive used furniture. An ugly color or
minor surface damage will pose no problem for
you as you do your magic makeover. This piece is
from the 1950s—small pieces from this period often have quirky charm that the larger items lack.
While the color combination might not be for ev-
eryone, it captures some of the airy feeling of the
original blond finish, but with an attitude.

This small, 1950s-style nightstand is an ideal candidate for a vinegar painted finish.

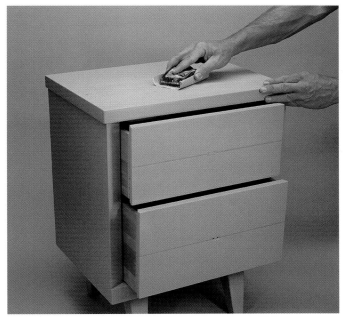

1 Remove the hardware and sand the entire piece with 150-grit sandpaper. Wipe clean with a tack cloth and prime the surface with gray primer. Use wood filler to fill small holes or abrasions that show up after priming and sand again with 220-grit sandpaper.

2 Wipe the surface clean and basecoat with Benjamin Moore #537 or a similar color.

YOU WILL NEED:

- Two-drawer nightstand
- Gray primer
- Benjamin Moore #537 or a similar color of base paint
- Prussian Blue vinegar paint
- Burnt Umber vinegar paint
- Burnt Sienna vinegar paint
- Wood filler
- 150- and 220-grit sandpaper
- #0000 steel wool or fine abrasive pad
- Tack cloth
- Ruler
- ⅛" (.3cm) automotive masking tape
- ¾" (1.9cm) drafting tape
- Razor blade
- No. 2 oval sash brush
- Glazing compound
- Small watercolor brush
- Plastic wrap
- 2-inch (5.1cm) foam brush
- Varnish and other finishing materials (see part four)

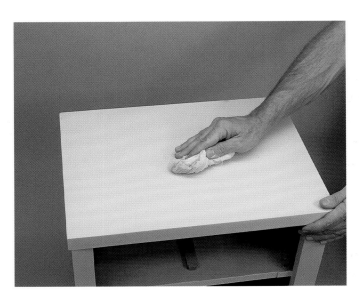

3 Sand lightly and wipe clean with a tack cloth. Recoat with the base color, if necessary.

4 Use a ruler to draw a straight line about ¾" (1.9cm) in from the edge of the top.

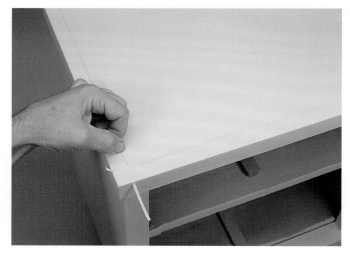

5 Apply ⅛" (.3cm) masking tape along the outside of the lines on all four sides. Burnish the tape with your thumbnail or some other smooth object. Trim the corners by pulling the tape up against a razor blade.

6 Apply ¾" (1.9cm) drafting tape on the inside of the ⅛" (.3cm) masking tape. Overlap the two tapes so there is no gap between them.

7 Repeat the taping process on the front of the drawers. Since each of my drawers has a horizontal groove in the center to suggest it is really two drawers, I've masked off four panels to reinforce this illusion.

8 Working around the perimeter of the top, lay in alternate areas of Prussian Blue and Burnt Umber.

9 Working quickly, stipple the colors together to create a wet-in-wet mixture. The colors can blend more in some areas than others, but they should not be pure in any one place.

10 When dry, apply one coat of varnish.

11 After the varnish dries on the border, remove the drafting tape from the inside area and place it over the painted border. Brush in a layer of Burnt Umber vinegar paint.

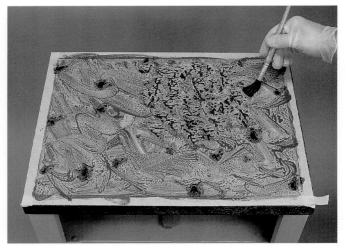

12 While the Burnt Umber is still wet, touch in spots of the Prussian Blue.

13 Stipple these colors together with the same technique you used in the border area. Work quickly so the paint will remain wet.

14 Texture this area with a piece of glazing compound. Move the compound in a series of arcs and curved lines until the entire top is completed.

15 When dry, apply one coat of varnish.

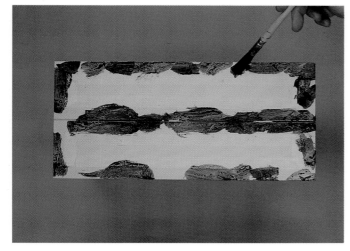

16 Using Prussian Blue and Burnt Umber, paint the borders of the drawers in the same fashion as the border on the top.

17 Stipple the colors together with the same technique you used before. When dry, apply one coat of varnish. Make sure to paint and varnish the ends of the drawers as you go along. When the varnish is dry, move the wide drafting tape so that it covers the painted borders.

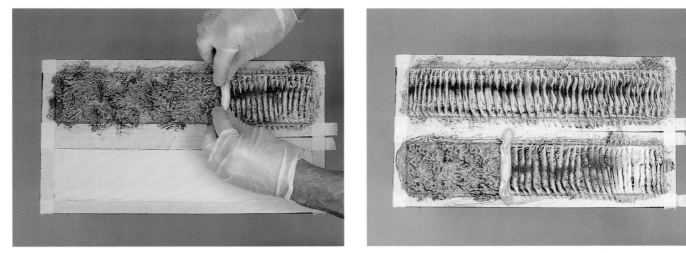

18 Paint the centers of the drawers similar to the top of the piece, but move the glazing compound in a straight line across the drawer. Apply one coat of varnish to each section before moving on to the next section.

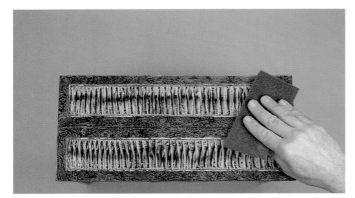

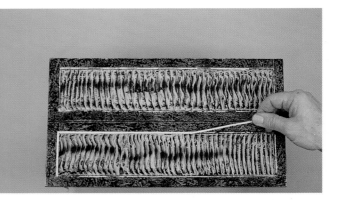

19 Remove the wide drafting tape and varnish the entire drawer front. Allow to dry. This would be a good time to rub down the finish with a #0000 steel wool pad or some other fine abrasive pad.

20 Remove the narrow masking tape from the drawers and apply at least one more coat of varnish to the surface.

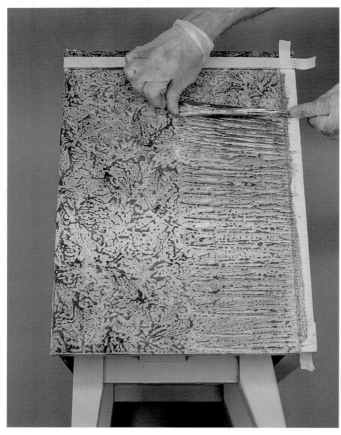

21 To paint the sides of the nightstand, follow steps 11-13, substituting Burnt Sienna for Burnt Umber. After stippling the Prussian Blue and Burnt Sienna press a piece of pleated plastic wrap into the paint in a series of wide rows. Keep in mind that this work has to be done with the surface in a horizontal position or the paint will run. Apply a coat of varnish to this area when it is dry.

22 Paint the legs by stippling and blending patches of Burnt Sienna and Prussian Blue. You may have to practice to get the correct paint consistency so the paint will not run down the sides of the legs. As always, varnish the areas before moving on to the next part of the piece.

23 Paint the front of the nightstand in the same way you did the sides, stippling Prussian Blue and Burnt Sienna together.

24 Then, dampen a 2-inch (5.1cm) foam brush with Burnt Umber paint and press it into the surface to create a series of stripes.

25 Work the stripes down each side and across the horizontal dividers. Apply one coat of varnish.

26 Remove the remaining tape and apply additional coats of varnish as needed to form a protective finish. Replace the hardware on the drawers to finish the project.

12

TWO-DOOR CABINET

S ometimes you will find a piece of furniture that is so simple it calls for a more
exuberant color or pattern. This small,
two-door cabinet falls into that category. Don't
be afraid to take a chance. A whole room of this
color and texture would be too much, but a small
touch sets off an otherwise sedate environment.

This simple, two-door storage cabinet has minor surface damage but is a good size and design for a vinegar paint project.

2 Use spackling and a putty knife to fill scratches and other surface imperfections. Sand the surface again after the spackling compound has dried, and wipe clean with a cloth dampened with naphtha or mineral spirits.

3 Prime the cabinet both inside and out with an ochre-tinted primer. When dry, sand with 150-grit sandpaper.

1 Remove the doors and hardware. Sand the entire piece, including the doors, with 120-grit sandpaper. This will clean and smooth the surface and will help to reveal areas that need to be filled.

4 Basecoat the piece with yellow ochre (Pigskin) latex or oil enamel and sand again with the 150-grit sandpaper. Give the piece a second coat of yellow ochre for a rich, even basecoat.

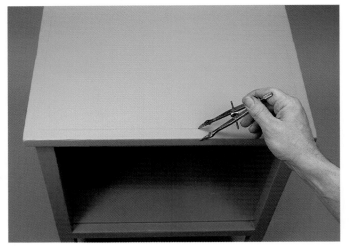

5 Use a compass to create a linear border along the edge of the top.

6 On the outside of this line, apply ⅛" (.3cm) masking tape and trim the corners by pulling it up against a razor blade.

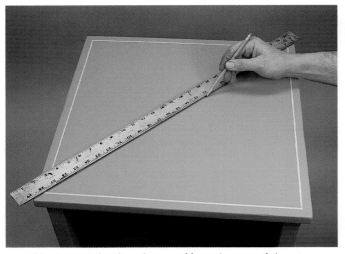

7 Using a straightedge, draw an X on the top of the piece.

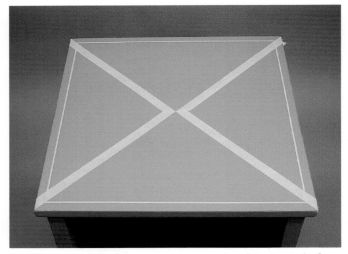

8 Then, using the X as a guideline, apply ¾" (1.9cm) drafting tape to create an hourglass shape. This taping technique allows you to create an inlaid effect without borders.

YOU WILL NEED:

- Two-door storage cabinet
- Ochre-tinted primer
- Yellow ochre (Pigskin) base paint
- Manganese Violet vinegar paint
- Prussian Blue vinegar paint
- Spackling and putty knife
- 120- and 150-grit sandpaper
- Cloth and naphtha or mineral spirits
- ⅛" (.3cm) automotive masking tape
- ¾" (1.9cm) drafting tape

- Painter's tape
- Razor blade or craft knife
- No. 2 oval sash brush
- Compass
- Straightedge and pencil
- Small watercolor brush
- 2-inch (5.1cm) and 3-inch (7.6cm) foam brushes
- Glazing compound
- Vinegar and cotton swab, if needed
- Varnish and other finishing materials (see part four)

9 Reinforce the drafting tape with wider painters' tape, then loosely brush Manganese Violet into one of the taped-off triangles.

10 Using a small watercolor brush, quickly lay in dots of Prussian Blue.

11 Moisten a 2-inch (5.1cm) foam brush with Manganese Violet and walk it through the Manganese Violet/Prussian Blue paint combination. Refer to pages 30-31 for more specific instructions regarding this technique. When dry, apply one coat of varnish.

12 Move to the other section of the hourglass shape and repeat the process. After the varnish has dried, remove the wide drafting tape and reposition it on the painted sections.

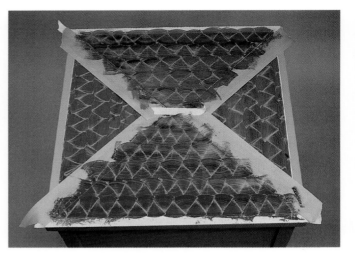

13 Place the tape so that a very thin line of the painted surface is visible. Otherwise, when the tape is removed a sliver of the basecolor will be present.

14 Paint and varnish the remaining two areas of the top by repeating the same technique.

15 Remove all the wide drafting tape to reveal the inlaid effect. After the center has dried, mask on the inside of the ⅛″ (.3cm) tape to protect the newly painted areas.

16 Freely brush in alternate bands of Manganese Violet and Prussian Blue around the border.

17 While the bands of color are still wet, stamp the border with a piece of glazing compound, pulling the colors together and creating a linear texture. You can try to do the edge at the same time or come back later and do it separately.

18 Varnish this area when dry. After the varnish has dried, remove the wide drafting tape, but leave the thin masking tape on the surface. Give the entire tabletop another coat of varnish to seal all the surfaces.

19 When the top has dried, peel up the ⅛″ (.3cm) masking tape to reveal the linear border.

20 If paint has leaked under the ⅛″ (.3cm) masking tape, use a cotton swab moistened with vinegar to remove it. Apply another coat of varnish to protect the linear details.

21 Tape off the doors using the masking tape to create a border. Overlap this tape with wide drafting tape. Paint the center panels using the same color and technique as on the top. When dry, apply one coat of varnish.

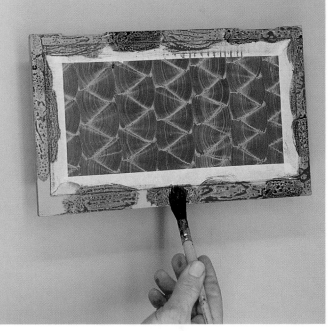

22 Move the wide drafting tape to the center of the panel and lay down alternate bands of Manganese Violet and Prussian Blue.

23 Instead of using the glazing compound, stipple this area with the no. 2 oval sash brush. Apply one coat of varnish to the border.

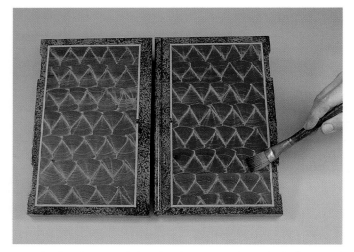

24 After the varnish has dried, remove the wide drafting and narrow masking tapes and give the doors another coat of varnish.

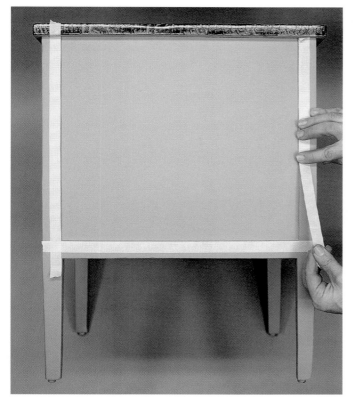

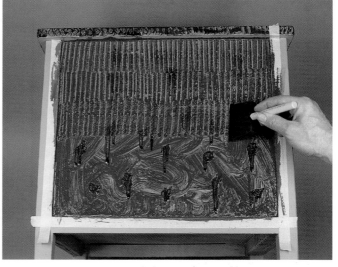

25 Turn the cabinet on its side and mask off the end panel with the wide drafting tape.

26 Use the same color combination as on the top, but texture it here by pressing into the paint with a 3-inch (7.6cm) foam brush, creating rows of parallel lines.

27 When the end panel has dried, move the drafting tape from the border to the painted surface. Paint and texture the raised structural areas with the same technique you used for the border on the top. Apply one coat of varnish to each section before you move on to the next section.

28 Continue the same texturing process on the legs, completing all four horizontal surfaces before moving on to another side of the cabinet.

29 Rotate the cabinet onto its back and continue texturing the legs and frame. Note: A piece of drafting tape protects the interior from paint drips. When every side has been textured and varnished, allow the piece to dry, and then replace the doors and hardware to complete your masterpiece.

PART FOUR

Finishing Your Vinegar Painted Furniture

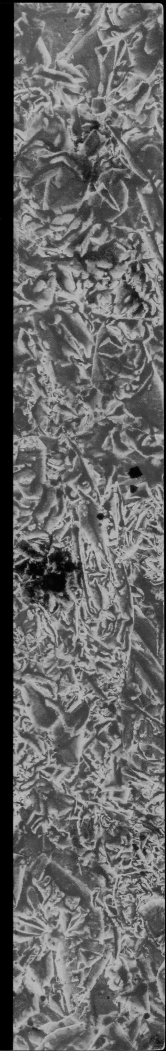

As mentioned in part one, there are several choices available to you in the finishing of your vinegar painted work. The most important thing to keep in mind is that since the vinegar paint is water-soluble, it must be sealed with a solvent-based coating. This will make your decorative work permanent and will provide a durable finish. Durability is especially important on furniture items that will receive daily use. At the same time, a smooth, lustrous finish will contribute to the clarity and brilliance of your textures and colors. Achieving these results is a combination of the finish you choose and the way you apply it.

Blanket Chest, 48" wide × 18" deep × 24" tall (1.2m × 45.7cm × 61cm), private collection

CHOOSING A FINISH

Oil-Based Varnish

Oil-based varnish, now also called alkyd, is the traditional finish for vinegar paint. This finish is a brushable, slightly amber-colored, transparent material that can be purchased in a variety of sheens:

- Flat varnish has practically no shine at all.
- Satin is one step up from flat.
- Semi-gloss varnish is slightly less shiny than gloss.
- Gloss varnish is very shiny.

In general, gloss varnish is tougher than flat varnish because silica, which is added to varnish to make it flat, weakens the film strength.

While you may prefer alkyd varnish because of its more traditional nature or handling characteristics, keep in mind it will take a long time to dry. While drying, the surface may gather dust, insects and fingerprints. The amber color becomes noticeable as you apply more coats and may cause an undesirable color shift in blues and pastels.

Polyurethane Varnish

Polyurethane varnish is a modern, solvent-based variation of traditional varnish in which the varnish film is composed of a plastic compound. Polyurethane is available in the same sheens as traditional varnish, has the same amber color and is also meant to be brushed on. However, it has two major advantages over traditional varnish: It dries much more quickly, and it forms a tougher protective film. Some people complain that polyurethane has a "plastic" look, but I have found that, if you apply the finish as directed by the manufacturer, the results are indistinguishable from conventional varnish. I strongly recommend polyurethane varnish to the students in my workshops.

Nitrocellulose Lacquer

Nitrocellulose lacquer is a third possibility for finishing vinegar paint. Unlike varnish, it dries almost instantly through the rapid evaporation of its solvent, lacquer thinner. Aside from its quick drying time, lacquer's main advantage is that it may be purchased in a formulation other than amber, so that no color shift occurs as it is applied over the base color and vinegar paint. This type of lacquer is referred to as "water white" or "butyrated." However, lacquer is difficult to brush on due to its rapid drying time, and it emits stronger fumes than varnish. For these reasons, it is usually sprayed on in a ventilated booth. I would recommend lacquer only if you are an experienced finisher, or if you have access to spray equipment and a professional spray booth. Lacquer thinner is a very strong solvent and can dissolve oil-based paints. Therefore, if you are considering using a lacquer finish, use only latex base color.

APPLYING THE FIRST COAT

After the vinegar paint has dried, apply the first coat of varnish very lightly to avoid disturbing the pattern. Any strong rubbing or scrubbing with the brush may dislodge particles of pigment and cause the paint to smudge; it's a good idea to thin the first coat of varnish with mineral spirits so it will flow on freely. This will also allow the varnish to thoroughly penetrate the pigment and bond it to the base paint. I thin the first coat by adding about 10 percent paint thinner to the varnish. This amount will vary depending on how thick the product is when you open the can. If it appears very thin already, you may not need to thin the varnish at all.

Your goal with this first coat is to lay on a consistent film of finish without missing any spots. The better your varnish brush, the more successful you will be. You will usually be working horizontally, so for the most part runs and sags should not be a problem.

Always be sure to apply the finish in a consistent direction, brushing to the very edge of the surface. Move around the work after you have finished to look for gaps or puddles. Take care of any problems immediately, because it will be much harder to make corrections once the varnish begins to set up. When you have completed the varnishing, wipe the excess varnish out of your brush and store the brush in paint thinner until you are ready to use it again.

This coat will dry faster because of the paint thinner. After the varnish is dry, scuff it lightly with an abrasive pad to remove dust particles that settled in the finish. Be sure to wipe the surface with a tack cloth afterward.

VARNISHING SMALL SECTIONS

If you are working with taped lines and will be switching colors from one side of the tape to the other, don't sand until you have vinegar painted the entire piece and are ready to build up the finish on the entire surface. It is safe to apply drafting tape to an area after the second coat of varnish has dried.

APPLYING THE SECOND COAT

The second coat of varnish will be full strength and should catch any holidays (small places you didn't put any finish) in the first coat. Follow the manufacturer's instructions to determine how long to wait between coats. If you try to recoat too soon, the new coat may attack and lift the previous layer. If you wait too long, the two layers may not bond well to each other. After the second coat dries, sand it very lightly with 280-grit sandpaper to diminish any brushstrokes and remove blemishes. Be careful not to sand through the finish! You only want to begin the smoothing process at this point.

APPLYING ADDITIONAL COATS

You may add as many coats as you feel necessary to provide a smooth, strong finish. If you want to apply additional coats of finish, but the recommended time frame for recoating has passed, sand the previous coat to create a tooth for the new coat of finish, as recommended above.

While two coats of varnish may be sufficient for decorative objects such as frames, I feel that three coats is the absolute minimum for any surface that will receive wear and tear. Four or five coats will provide a stronger finish, especially for surfaces such as tabletops or other high-stress areas. It is important to sand after every coat has dried to remove dust particles and brush marks from the finish. If

you don't, the varnish will become very rough, obscuring the patterning and colors of your vinegar painting.

FINISHING THE FINISH

After the last coat of varnish has dried, you will still need to rub out the finish to make it as smooth as possible. I think a #0000 steel wool pad is the best rubbing agent for a vinegar painted surface. As with sanding, you want to work in long, smooth strokes with a consistent pressure on the steel wool pad. You will get better results if you lubricate the pad while rubbing. The best lubricant is one especially designed for this purpose, such as Behlen's Wool Lube which will give you a silky-smooth, satin finish.

Paste wax may also be used to lubricate the steel wool. Instead of applying wax with a cloth, use the finest steel wool. This process will give you a slightly shinier result, since the wax can be buffed to a soft sheen when you have finished rubbing. You may also apply the wax with a cloth after you have rubbed the varnish with the wool lubricant. This will result in a beautiful, lustrous surface.

After you have finished varnishing, sanding and rubbing, you may still see irregularities in the finish due to the texturing of the vinegar paint. You could eliminate even this unevenness, but since this is part of what creates the finish, I find it actually adds to the charm of the work.

Wrapping the sandpaper around a sanding block ensures a more even finish. Sanding blocks are available in a variety of materials, or you can make your own from a piece of wood. My favorite is made of cork. The backside of a sheet of sandpaper will show the grit number and other information about the paper. Finer grades of sandpaper have higher grit numbers. As you build up coats of varnish, sand between coats with increasingly finer grades. I usually end up sanding with 400-grit sandpaper before the final coat of varnish. Wet sanding with special paper made for this purpose gives a smoother result and helps to keep the sandpaper from clogging.

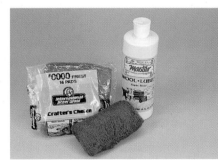

After the final coat of varnish, rub out the finish with #0000 steel wool and a product called Wool Lube. This will impart a silky-feeling, satin finish to your work. Always rub and sand in long, horizontal strokes in the direction of the grain. Be careful not to rub through edges or corners.

For a final layer of protection and luster, give your piece a coat of light-colored paste wax. Wax the bottoms of drawers and the insides of doorframes to provide smooth movement of sliding parts and to lessen wear and tear from friction.

Appendix

TROUBLESHOOTING

Here is a list of problems you might encounter, along with their most likely causes and solutions. They are arranged according to the painting process.

Preparation
Problem: Sandpaper gets clogged.
Cause: Surface is waxed, dirty or deteriorated.
Solutions: (1) clean surface with naphtha and #00 steel wool before sanding; (2) use a coarser grade of sandpaper; or (3) have the piece chemically stripped.

Priming and Basecoating
Problem: Dried paint leaves coarse brush marks.
Cause: The paint dried before it "flowed out" or became level.
Solutions: (1) thin primer with appropriate solvent; (2) apply less paint; (3) brush out paint in the direction of the wood grain before it begins to set up; (4) use a better-quality brush; or (5) sand between each coat to minimize the problem.

Taping
Problem: Tape buckles or flips when applied to curves.
Cause: Tension on the tape is insufficient.
Solution: Stretch the tape as you press it down.

Problem: Paint leaks under tape or tape comes up when vinegar paint is applied.
Cause: Tape has not made consistent contact with the surface.
Solutions: (1) burnish the tape after you apply it, and pay particular attention to overlaps and the inside of curves; or (2) if the problem persists, apply a thin coat of the base color over the taped surface to seal the edges of the tape.

Problem: Tape pulls up the paint when removed.
Cause: Adhesion between tape and paint is greater than between paint and original surface.
Solutions: (1) clean original surface before applying primer; (2) remove the tape as soon as possible; (3) peel the tape up very slowly and stop if paint begins to come off; (4) remove the tape from the opposite end; or (5) instead of pulling the tape up, try pushing or rolling it off.

Vinegar Painting
Problem: Latex base paint begins to dissolve when the vinegar paint is applied.
Cause: Base paint has not dried thoroughly or the vinegar paint has remained wet for too long.
Solutions: (1) wait for the base paint to cure before applying the vinegar paint; (2) work more quickly so the surface doesn't remain wet for too long; (3) switch brands or grades of paint; or (4) use alkyd base paint.

Problem: Vinegar paint beads up or doesn't hold a pattern.
Cause: Surface tension of the vinegar paint prevents it from flowing onto the basecoat.

Solutions: (1) use a less glossy base paint; (2) push harder on the brush while scrubbing the vinegar paint onto the surface; (3) degloss the base paint with a fine abrasive pad; (4) add more pigment to the vinegar paint; or (5) add a little more detergent to the vinegar paint.

Problem: Vinegar paint completely covers the base color.
Cause: Vinegar paint is too thick.
Solution: Add more vinegar medium to the paint.

Problem: Vinegar paint dries out before you can complete the pattern.
Cause: Surface area is too large for the available working time of the paint.
Solutions: (1) have all your materials ready before you begin so you can work more quickly; (2) apply the vinegar paint to a portion of the surface, texture it, then move on to the next portion; (3) re-moisten the surface with a spray bottle filled with vinegar; (4) subdivide the surface with tape so you can work in smaller areas; or (5) get a helper to apply the paint so you can follow behind and concentrate on texturing.

Varnishing
Problem: Applying the varnish disturbs the pattern of the vinegar paint.
Causes: Vinegar paint is still wet, or too much pressure or scrubbing is used with the varnish brush.
Solutions: (1) make sure the vinegar paint is totally dry—use a hair dryer to speed up drying; (2) apply the varnish in one direction using a high-quality varnish brush; or (3) thin the varnish with mineral spirits if it's very thick so it will flow more easily.

Problem: Varnish attacks the underlying varnish or alkyd base paint and causes it to crinkle.
Cause: Solvents in the varnish dissolve the uncured material beneath it.
Solutions: (1) if you see this beginning to happen, stop varnishing immediately and let the varnish dry—you may be able to sand away small imperfections; (2) give the alkyd base paint or varnish time to cure, not just dry to the touch; or (3) use latex base paint.

Problem: The varnish develops runs and sags while drying.
Cause: Too much varnish was applied to the surface.
Solutions: (1) apply a thinner coat of varnish by getting less on the brush; (2) check varnished areas carefully for excess before the varnish dries; or (3) after the varnish dries, sand off most of the run, but be careful not to sand through into the vinegar paint.

Problem: Varnish attacks the drafting tape, making it messy to remove.
Cause: Some "quick-dry" varnishes and sealers have unusual solvents that dissolve the adhesive material on tape.
Solution: Use only standard polyurethane or alkyd varnish. If you are tempted to try a "quick-dry" product, experiment on a sample board first.

Problem: The varnish is pulled up when the tape is removed.
Causes: Coats of varnish have not bonded to each other, or the

varnish is so thick it won't separate along the edge of the tape.
Solutions: (1) sand between coats of varnish so there is good adhesion of each coat to the one below; (2) remove the tape after two coats of varnish when possible; or (3) if you have applied several coats of varnish before you remove the tape, it may be helpful to cut along the edge of the tape with a craft knife before you pull it up. This will help prevent the tape from pulling up the surrounding varnish.

Problem: When sanding between coats of varnish, the vinegar paint is sanded away in spots, revealing the base color.
Cause: The sandpaper is removing all the varnish and attacking the vinegar paint.
Solutions: (1) apply at least two coats of varnish before sanding; (2) don't sand so aggressively—just smooth the surface slightly; (3) use a finer-grit sandpaper; or (4) switch to fine steel wool, which will remove less varnish.

SOURCES FOR MATERIALS

A Good Paint Store
Somewhere in Your Area
A good paint store should carry more than one brand of paint. It should also stock sanding and finishing supplies, steel wool, thinners, paint additives, brushes, spackling paste, glazing compound and painting tools. If you're lucky, the owner or manager will be knowledgeable about mixing paint and paint technology.

Automotive Paint Supply
Look in the Yellow Pages under "Automobile, body and paint supplies," or ask your local body shop where they get their paint. This is where you will get the ⅛" (.3cm) masking tape for the thin masked lines. I recommend the standard paper-based tape over plastic tape. Either one is fine for straight lines, but the paper tape adheres better to curved lines.

Bill Russell Studio
1215 Frankford Ave.
Philadelphia, PA 19125
(215) 238-9669
A Vinegar Paint Finishing Kit is available for $55.00 (includes shipping and handling and tax). It contains a picture frame, paints, varnish, tools and instructions for creating your own mini-masterpiece. It's a great way to get yourself or a friend off and running with vinegar painting. Spring and fall workshops in various decorative painting techniques are also available. Call or write for a schedule of upcoming workshops.

Constantine's Woodworking
2050 Eastchester Rd.
Bronx, NY 10461
(800) 223-8087
Constantine's has tools, hardware and finishing supplies for woodworkers and furniture restorers. They carry the striping tool for applying the thin lines of paint, as well as many other hard-to-find items.

Daniel Smith Art Supplies
4150 First Ave. South
P.O. Box 84268
Seattle, WA 98124-5568
(800) 426-7923
This is a good general art supply source. They have good prices on their own brand of dry pigments. Quick and courteous telephone service is an added bonus.

Garrett Wade
161 Avenue of the Americas
New York, NY 10013
(800) 221-2942
This company offers high-quality woodworking and finishing supplies.

Kremer Pigments
228 Elizabeth St.
New York, NY 10012
(212) 219-2394
This is the ultimate pigment source. Thirteen kinds of black! They're also a good source for other unusual painting materials and tools. The catalog may be a bit daunting for the beginner, but the representatives are very helpful over the phone.

Mohawk Finishing Products
Rt. 30 North
Amsterdam, NY 12010
(800) 545-0047
Here are supplies for professional finishers; if it's used in wood finishing, this company probably carries it.

Muralo Paint Corp. and Elder Jenks Brushes
148 E. Fifth St.
Bayonne, NJ 07002
(800) 631-3440
These are the manufacturers of the "Ultra" line of waterbased paints that perform similarly to alkyd paints. They also produce high-quality, natural-bristle no. 2 oval sash brushes. Their representatives should be able to help you find a source in your area for their products.

3M Corporation
(800) 364-3577 (Helpline)
3M manufactures a green sandpaper specially formulated for sanding latex paint. Look for it at paint stores that carry other 3M products, or call the helpline and tell them you are looking for a source for product #84082.

Wood Worker's Supply
1108 N. Glenn Rd.
Casper, WY 82601
(800) 645-9292
This company carries varnishes, a small selection of pigments, rubbing compounds (including Behlen's Wool Lube) and other unusual products for finishing, including 3M green sandpaper.